"[Knipfel's] grouchy. He drinks too much. I
And, boy, do we love him by the end of
seamless blend of tragedy (he has a brain le
and comedy (he'd rather smack into poles than use a cane)."
—*Entertainment Weekly*

"HILARIOUS . . . reads like an absurdist manifesto."
—*San Francisco Chronicle*

"An extraordinary emotional ride. It is maniacally aglow with a born storyteller's gifts of observation and an amiably deranged sense of humor . . . What begins as a cautionary tale turns out to be an exemplary American life. The Park Service ought to be charging admission. Long may Knipfel continue to astonish us." —*Thomas Pynchon*

"The author writes of his maladies with such festive panache we follow his journey from squinty kid to cane-wielding grown-up with a combination of horror at the hand he was dealt and admiration for the savage grace with which he ultimately embraced it."
—*Mirabella*

"Illuminating . . . Most of Knipfel's memories focus on his dozen or so post-college years, a time when his marriage was failing, his visual field was shrinking, and an inoperable tumor in his brain was giving him seizures and suicidal depression. While this may sound like the makings of a dreary and pitiful tale of woe, it is anything but. Knipfel's bizarre antics with his unconventional friends and his sometimes surrealistic encounters with doctors, nurses, social workers, small-time criminals, subway riders, and bar denizens provoke laughter, not tears . . . sharp and wickedly funny."
—*Kirkus Reviews* (starred review)

"Insightful . . . Knipfel musters his best laughs at his own expense."
—*New York Post*

"Knipfel brilliantly realizes human nature in a series of quiet observations . . . For the sighted, it's hard to imagine what the blind really give up, but Knipfel reminds his readers with startling clarity."
—*The Capital Times*

"Knipfel's caustic voice is certainly welcome in the crowded world of the cheaply 'life-affirming' live-to-tell-all."
—*Atlanta Journal and Constitution*

(*continued on next page*)

s l a c k j a w

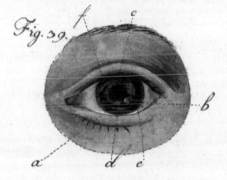

j i m   k n i p f e l

BERKLEY BOOKS, NEW YORK

Portions of this book, in different form,
have appeared previously in the following publications:
Browbeat, *Castaways*, *Hootenanny*, *New York Press*,
Scalawags, *So What*, and *Welcomat*.

Some names have been changed in deference to friends and subjects.

SLACKJAW

A Berkley Book / published by arrangement with
Jeremy P. Tarcher

PRINTING HISTORY
Jeremy P. Tarcher / Putnam edition / February 1999
Berkley trade paperback edition / February 2000

The Penguin Putnam Inc. World Wide Web site address is
http://www.penguinputnam.com

ISBN: 0-425-17330-5

BERKLEY®
Berkley Books are published by The Berkley Publishing Group,
a division of Penguin Putnam Inc.,
375 Hudson Street, New York, New York 10014.
BERKLEY and the "B" design are trademarks
belonging to Penguin Putnam Inc.

PRINTED IN THE UNITED STATES OF AMERICA

10 9 8 7 6 5 4 3 2 1

For my parents,
George and Janice Knipfel,
who have never once given up hope,
even after I have, time and again.
I love them with all I have

contents

introduction

MY GRANDMA MYRT DIED when I was twelve years old.
She had been battling the ravages of cancer far too long, until one
Thanksgiving morning she lost the fight.

In a hushed, dim funeral home in Baldwin, Wisconsin, I spent
an afternoon navigating a crowd of family and strangers, until I
found myself a spot in an uncomfortable straight-backed chair
against a wall. I sat down, not knowing what I was supposed to
do. It was the first funeral I had ever attended.

Across the room, I saw my uncle Tom, my mom's brother. I
saw his beer belly, crooked tie, sideburns, and thick glasses working their way through the crowd toward me. I assumed Uncle
Tom was going to repeat the same simple words of consolation
everyone else had been saying, but I was wrong.

Uncle Tom looked down at me sitting on that chair with the
scratchy floral-patterned seat and didn't say hello, didn't say anything, except, "You better start learning Braille now."

"Thanks, Uncle Tom," I replied, deciding to avoid him for the
rest of the afternoon. Longer, if possible.

All I knew about my uncle Tom was that his eyes were worse
than mine. I didn't know that we both suffered from the same
disease, and I wouldn't know for many years to come. The way I
figured it, as big as our extended family was, it just made sense.
It was the bad luck of the draw that two of us would need glasses.
Back in 1977 nobody talked about genetics much, at least not at
funerals in small Wisconsin towns. And nobody then could have

predicted that the world would go dark on me while I was still a reasonably young man.

Most of the sophisticates might sneer at my uncle for living in a trailer, watching professional wrestling on television, and drinking Pabst Blue Ribbon; but he wasn't a stupid man. He was right on the money when it came to my eyesight.

Having read plenty of those "Oh my God, I've got a horrible disease!" books over the years, I've been struck by something I most definitely did not want to do when it came to writing one of my own. In nearly all of these books, somewhere around a third of the way through, the author breaks away from the story to give a boring, clinical description of the disease in question. It's like the author of a cheap novel suddenly going into great detail about the history of landscape architecture, say, or shoe repair, to show us that he's done his research and really knows what the protagonist does for a living. That sort of thing pisses me off.

So, in order to avoid any awkward bumps in what those in the business call "narrative flow," I'd like to take a moment here to explain what my disease is all about.

The retina is the tissue that covers the back of the eye and contains the photoreceptor cells—the rods and cones. The cones are collected in the center of the retina, the macula, and are responsible for central and color vision. The rods are spread out around the macula and take care of peripheral and night vision. The rods and cones both are responsible for turning the light that comes in through the pupil into electrical impulses, which are then sent through the optic nerve to the brain, where "seeing" actually occurs.

"Retinitis pigmentosa," RP for short, is the snappy collective name given to a wide range of genetically linked diseases that attack the rods and cones, causing their breakdown and degeneration. I myself have what's known as "classical RP." What that

means is that from the moment I was born, the rods in my retinas started dissolving, while the cones remained relatively stable.
The first noticeable result was the loss of night vision. Then came
a creeping tunnel vision. While these symptoms grew worse and
more debilitating, my central vision, though limited, held. At
least for a while. The final result for most cases of RP is, obviously, blindness.

Research has been conducted for several decades, but at this
writing there is no cure for RP. It's untreatable and irreversible--
which essentially means that I'm shit out of luck.

On top of that, I discovered in my mid-twenties that I had a
lesion on the left temporal lobe of my brain, which, unbeknownst
to me, had been driving me, slowly but recklessly, toward madness for much of my life. That, too, was inoperable.

The numbers add up to a little more than nothing. It's estimated that 100,000 Americans suffer from some form of RP. It's
also estimated that, every year, 167,000 people in this country
suffer traumatic brain injuries that result in lesions like mine.
Those numbers themselves aren't all that remarkable, until you
put them together. The chance of having both conditions is along
the lines of 1 in 65,000, or about one-quarter of one-tenth of one
percent of the population.

There, see? Imagine how awful it would've been if I had
dropped that in the middle of a sex scene! Now that we know
what we're dealing with, I can get on with telling my stupid little
story.

—JMK
Brooklyn, 1998

Why do I need my eyes more than another?
It seems to me they never focused anything.
I console myself purely and simply with the thought.

—SAMUEL BECKETT

In a dark time, the eye begins to see.

—THEODORE ROETHKE

s l a c k j a w

*the world
is your oyster*

"SUICIDE HOTLINE?" the chipper young woman on the other end of the phone seemed to ask me when she answered.

When I dialed the phone, I had no idea what I was going to say. I hadn't thought that far ahead. What: "I'm about to open my veins. Now what the hell are you gonna do about it?" That wouldn't do. I get into trouble when I don't think about things beforehand. I've never been a good improviser. So instead of saying something moronic, I opted to say nothing at all.

"Hello?" the voice at the other end returned. "Anyone there?"

All the Nietzsche I had been immersed in went right out the window.

"Hello?" she asked again. "I can hear you *breeaathing!*"

"Shut up," I snapped. I was tempted to say, "That's it, you blew it," and hang up, but I wasn't that cruel, yet.

"So what's goin' on?"

"Oh, what do you think? That I just called to chat?"

"I *meant,* what are you planning?" She meant business.

"Razors. I guess. At least that's what I have in front of me."

"Razors rarely work, you know."

Terrific, I call for help, and I get someone who critiques my style.

"Got any better suggestions? I can't afford a gun."

"That's not what I'm here for. I'm here to help."

"Well, you're doing a bang-up job of it."

[1]

"Hey," she said, "we got off on the wrong foot." I could hear the exasperation in her voice. "Let's start again. What's your name?"

"Name doesn't matter."

"Okay," she said. "Why don't you tell me why you want to kill yourself?"

"A man has to have a reason? I didn't break up with a girl-friend, I didn't lose a job, and I wasn't just told that I have Hodgkin's disease. Nothing that simple."

I didn't have an answer to her question. I had begun to no-tice that my failing eyesight—which in the past had affected me only at night—now was affecting me in the daytime as well. I couldn't cut it in physics, I couldn't cut it at the University of Chicago. So here I was in Madison, at the University of Wiscon-sin, a nondescript state school that would admit autistics if they could pay the tuition, studying philosophy, which wouldn't do me a damn bit of good in the future. Those facts weren't reason enough, either.

"Any possible reasons you could give me?"

I was in it now. I might as well try. "I guess you could say I'm a fuck-up."

"Yeah?" Her voice dropped to a throaty whisper. She must have thought that she was getting someplace, that she had finally broken through. "When was the last time you fucked up?"

"About five minutes ago, when I picked up the phone to call you."

"That's not very nice." She was attempting to hold on to her sincerity.

"Sorry," I said. I suppose I was, too, a little.

"Let's try something else. Let's turn things around. Tell me some of the things you like."

I thought for a minute.

"I'm pretty hard-pressed to come up with anything just at this very moment, ma'am."

"C'mon, there must be something. You must have friends."

"Nope."

"None at all?"

"Nope."

"What about your family?"

"My family's cool. I've got nothing but kind things to say about them."

"There, you see? Can you imagine how they would feel if you killed yourself?"

"So, what, I should go on living solely out of guilt? Guilt over how they would feel if I were to end it? That's not much to work with." I chuckled.

"See? You just laughed! If you laugh, that must mean something. Everything's not completely dark."

"Well, Wagner said," I responded, one more young man who took his Wagner too seriously, " 'Amidst laughter should we face our doom.' "

"Who?"

"Never mind," I told her, knowing the whole thing was a mistake. It wasn't going anywhere, and never would go anywhere. "Thanks for taking the time, but I'm suddenly real tired. I'm going to bed."

"Are you still thinking about hurting yourself?"

"Well, yeah. But right now I'm just too damn tired." These few minutes on the phone with her had completely sapped what energy I had left. She began to say something else, but I hung up. Useless. I lay down on my mattress, still dressed, and fell asleep.

The next morning was brisk and clear outside. There were things I was supposed to be doing, but for the life of me, I couldn't remember what. I put on my hat and coat, left the apartment, and started walking in a direction I'd never gone. I had started wearing a black fedora everywhere when I was sixteen years old. At the time, I thought it made me look like Bogart. I was mistaken. So many of us go through life trying to be Bogart or Cagney, but we mostly end up like Elisha Cook, Jr. I certainly did. But the hat stayed. It was my most identifiable feature.

I walked for hours, hoping I could exhaust myself and walk the bad thoughts out of my head. Once my legs started getting numb, I turned around and started back home. While I walked, I took inventory, only to discover that there was nothing to count.

When I got home, I opened the door, threw my hat and coat on the mattress, snatched the razors off the desk, took them into the bathroom, and searched in vain for a comfortable spot on the tiled floor. After a few minutes I gave up on that silly notion and set to work on the right wrist.

I KNEW THE JIG WAS UP when I heard a knock on the door. I was on my knees over the toilet. There was blood everywhere, on the floor, on the toilet seat, smeared on the walls. The puddle of water in the toilet was dark red. I stared down at my arm and saw the razor blade sticking out of the deep wet maw that used to be my wrist.

I had blown it again. It looked as if I was going to live. To make things worse, it was my upstairs neighbor Steve at the door.

I stood slowly. I hadn't lost enough blood to be light-headed, but my knees were shaky. I leaned against the wall, pulled the blade out of my wrist, and dropped it into the sink. Now there was blood in the sink. I stepped out of the bathroom and went to the door, where Steve was still knocking, and pressed my forehead against it.

"Steve," I said without opening, "things are kind of a mess in here. . . ."

"But things are *always* a mess in there," he said back.

"This is . . . different."

There was silence.

"Steve, I hurt myself in here. I want you to be prepared."

There was more silence. "Okay," he finally said.

I turned the lock and opened the door. He saw the blood on my shirt and looked at my arms.

"You don't want to see the bathroom."

Steve, who'd always been sort of motherly, stepped past me into the apartment. "I don't imagine you have any bandages," he said. "Do you have any paper towels?"

"Sink . . . under the . . . you know," I gestured feebly. Steve went to the sink, bent down, grabbed the roll of paper towels and ripped some off.

"Here, wrap those up. I'm taking you to the hospital. Put on your coat."

I slid into my trench coat, and Steve grabbed my army jacket and led me into the hallway. I gave him my keys, he locked the door, and we stepped outside.

There was a hospital five or six blocks away. Steve held my arm as we walked to the emergency room, the paper towels soaked and dripping a trail on the sidewalk.

It was a slow night in the emergency room, so it wasn't long before we were seated in front of a young woman who typed my vital statistics and insurance information into her computer.

"How did it happen?" she asked. Neither Steve nor I said anything.

"How did it happen?" She looked up from her screen. Steve glanced at me nervously and gave me a nudge.

"Fishing accident," I said.

She stared at me hard.

"Okay, it wasn't a fishing accident." I held up both arms. "What do you think it was?"

After she was finished with me, she told us to sit in the waiting room, where someone would come for me.

Wooden trains and stuffed animals were piled in one corner of the room. The walls were covered with lurid paintings of cartoon bunnies and cows. Everything was bright and happy. We were in there alone, and after a few moments I began to giggle.

Steve looked at me, frightened. "What?"

I pointed at the wall. "The bunnies."

Soon I was hysterical, shaking in my chair while the blood dried on my arms. Maybe it was the spooky euphoria that follows survival of a life-threatening experience. Maybe it was the horrifying laughter of a madman who simply didn't care anymore. But at the time, everything around me seemed silly. Steve was laughing just as hard as I was.

After we had waited laughing for twenty minutes, a tall woman came into the room and sat next to us.

"I was afraid you had left," she said kindly. "You were supposed to be next door, in the adults' waiting room."

She asked to see my arms. I pulled back the blood-soaked sleeves of my trench coat. My wrists were a clotted mess.

"Let's get that cleaned up." She left the room and returned with alcohol, cotton balls, and bandages. As she wiped the blood away, she explained that she was a social worker from the psych ward upstairs, where I would be spending the next few days.

She asked some more basic questions: Had I tried before, did I know why I did it, did I have a shrink. Before leaving to get things ready for me upstairs, she wrapped a bandage around my now clean wounds.

"Just keep those on, keep things covered up. We wouldn't want anything noxious falling into your wrists."

The idea of something noxious dropping off the ceiling into my wounds set Steve and me to laughing again as we waved good-bye to the social worker.

"Did you want to go to the adult waiting room?" Steve asked.

"Oh, why bother?"

Steve agreed, and there we sat and chuckled until an orderly arrived with a wheelchair to take me to be sewn up.

"Can I ride in the wheelchair?" Steve asked him.

"Are you hurt?"

"No, I just like wheelchairs."

"Then you can't."

I took my seat, and the orderly pushed me down the hall to an examination room, Steve tagging along behind.

"Get up on the table," the orderly said when we got to the room. "The doctor will be in here in a minute."

I crawled onto the crinkly paper, lay back, and waited. Steve wandered around the room, studying the tongue depressors and the blood pressure contraption on the wall.

When the doctor came in, he wouldn't look me in the eye. Graying beard, balding on top, glasses, stethoscope around his neck, officious.

"That was a stupid thing to do," he said.

"A happy hello to you, too," I answered.

He didn't say anything, just rooted around in some drawers. After he found what he was searching for, he turned to me. He held something in his hand. "First, I'm going to poke you with a pin," he said.

"What, as punishment?" Steve started to laugh, but swallowed it when the doctor shot him a glance.

"I'm going to poke you with this pin," he repeated, "to see if you caused yourself any nerve damage."

The rest of the time we were with him, I didn't say anything, except for yes and no. He didn't find any nerve damage, so he sewed up both wrists.

"You can go back out to the waiting room now," he said, still not looking me in the eye. "Someone will come and get you shortly." He paused. "Maybe someone upstairs can help you." With that encouragement and my wrists newly wrapped, I went out to wait again with Steve. It was well past midnight, but he stayed with me, and kept talking, and kept me laughing. When two social workers showed up to take me to the psych ward, he tagged along again, and they let him.

"I just want to see where you'll be putting him," Steve explained.

The four of us got on an elevator, and one of the women pulled out a key that gave access to the sixth floor. The women showed me to a room near the bank of elevators, with a single bed, a table beside it with a lamp on top, and a window. No roommate, thank God. They let Steve see the room and then informed him he had to leave.

I thanked him for his help and shook his hand before one of the women led him to the elevator. The woman who stayed had me clean out my pockets to make sure I wasn't carrying any sharps. She took the pen I had and handed me an awful, wrinkly bathrobe. Then she told me to sit on the bed and answer a few questions for her.

She pulled out a form several pages long and set to work. "What is your name?" she asked. "Do you know who the president is? Do you know where you are?"

It was way past my bedtime. I just wanted to sleep, but I answered her questions the best I could. When she asked me to count backward from a hundred by sevens, I had to protest.

"I'll give it a shot," I said, "but it's late and I'm real tired."

"We still have a ways to go. If you'd come in sooner, we wouldn't be doing this at two in the morning."

I answered her questions and let her read me my rights as an incarcerated loon, and signed the bottom of the form. Then she told me she was going to give me a tour of the ward.

"I really don't care to take a tour now, ma'am," I said. "Can't we do this tomorrow?"

"We have to do it tonight. I'm not going to be here tomorrow."

I slid off the bed and followed her into the hallway. Things were quiet, all the other doors were shut, but down the hall I saw a young woman sitting on the floor, knees to her chest, rocking back and forth against the wall.

"Don't mind her," my guide said. "That's Missy. Missy does that."

She showed me the communal bathrooms and showers. "You can use these in the morning," she explained.

I don't think so, I thought.

She showed me into the kitchen and opened the refrigerator door. A brown-yellow light shone on its sad contents. Food for the insane.

"You can have anything in here to eat. Except that piece of pie." She pointed at a piece of runny chocolate cream pie on a paper plate on the bottom shelf. "That's Bubba's pie."

I looked at that pie and remembered that I hadn't eaten anything since the morning. My head hurt worse than my wrists.

The woman led me back to my room, told me that someone would come talk to me in the morning, and wished me a good night. Then she closed the door.

I took off my clothes and put on that damn bathrobe and got in between the scratchy psych ward sheets. I lay there for a while, feeling my stomach and my head and my wrists, then got out of bed and sneaked into the hallway. There were no guards around, no orderlies. Just Missy. I tiptoed past her to the kitchen, where I ate Bubba's pie.

THE HOSPITAL LET ME OUT a few days later, with a promise from me that I would start seeing a shrink. I went through the phone book, but the doctors all looked expensive. I asked around among people I knew, and they suggested the university might offer some cut-rate service.

I wound up assigned to a shrink named Gerry. Seeing him required a mile-and-a-half walk from my apartment to the university hospital, where he had an office hidden away in the basement. Gerry was a short, fat, fuzzy man. A grad student working on his Ph.D., who saw me for cheap. Twice a week, negotiating with my class schedule, I made the trek to the hospital and sat in his office while he chain-smoked, nodded, and took notes. And I talked.

I had never been much of a talker, but things unspoken started spilling out, and Gerry took them seriously. He didn't blame my parents for all my troubles. They were innocent here, they never gave me anything but love, and I wasn't about to sit by while someone badmouthed them.

And he didn't.

I could feel my personality mutating in a radical way. I wasn't the silent, smart kid anymore. I had reopened Dosto-evsky's *Notes from Underground* and found that his narrator was speaking all the things that had been pounding through my head—the paranoia, the rage, the isolation, the fear.

I tried to explain this to Gerry. While I would make reference to "the Underground Man" to characterize this personality shift, he insisted on calling it the "Under-the-ground Man."

"I'm not dead yet," I pointed out.

Gerry never did get that name business right, so at our last meeting, four months after our first, I gave him a copy of the book and told him that only by reading it would shrinks like him ever be able to understand people like me.

Before I gave him the book, though, Gerry said something that cemented a change of attitude in me. It saved my life time and again over the next few years—and almost ended it just as often.

"Jim," he said, grinding out his last cigarette as we wrapped up, "you are not a terrible person. But the world is a terrible, *horrible* place. What you've got to do is take all that rage and all that hatred that's inside of you and turn it around. You've got to stop trying to destroy yourself. Turn that rage outward, go out and try to destroy the *world* instead."

Something in me, some high brick wall, crumbled at that moment, some heavy force floated out of me. On the way back to my apartment that bitter cold January evening, I balled up my gloved fist and punched it through a series of windows in an abandoned warehouse. I was starting to feel much better. "Die at the right time," Nietzsche wrote. At that moment, I did.

e x p o s u r e

I am five years old. It's a beautiful blue, cloudless summer day. I'm in the backyard, playing by myself (as usual), hanging upside down by my knees from the crossbar on the rickety, potentially deadly swing set. I reach up, grab hold of the bar, and drop myself to the ground—all short pants, button-down shirt, horn-rims, and crew cut—then run across the yard toward the back door of the small beige duplex we are living in. It's time for lunch.

EVEN IN THE WORST OF LIVES, lives in which it seems nothing has gone as planned, when everything's become a shambles, there are moments, bright and lucid moments, which for some reason that is never clear at the time, remain with us forever. Good moments when, for only an instant in the Big Mess, everything seems right.

I'm not talking about the big things—birth, marriage, moving to a new home, making a money deal. I'm talking about the most infinitesimal of moments—tiny facets in the diamond of larger experience, things nobody else would notice or remember five minutes after they passed. Instants. Secular epiphanies, barren of precedent or result.

I remember my childhood in these terms, but I remember the bad moments as well as the good. In memory splinters of joy and mild horror. Maybe that's because my mind has been shattered so many times and by so many forces over the years. Sometimes it seems these splinters—these little stories—are all I have left. But we measure our lives, and our lives are measured by others, in terms of the stories we can tell.

Although I tried hard to be a good kid, somehow I was nothing but trouble from the beginning. I was a breech birth and slid into the world with the umbilical cord wrapped around my neck. I'm still convinced I did that myself. When I was less than a year old, I had to start wearing braces on my twisted legs, which made it easier for my sister, Mary, to push me down when I was learning to walk. I also tended to trip over things and run into walls more than other children. Most of my baby pictures reveal a pudgy child with a too large head and a perpetual wide-eyed terror on his face.

My folks discovered I needed glasses when I was three years old. While they were trying to teach me how to read, I would snatch the books from them and hold the pages flush against my face to make sense of the words and pictures. They took me to see the eye doctor at K. I. Sawyer Air Force Base, where my father was stationed, in Michigan's Upper Peninsula. After a series of tests, the doctor broke the news that I was nearsighted.

"*Obscenely* nearsighted," he said, adding enigmatically that my eyeballs themselves were "shaped funny." I entered into consciousness a freak.

Riding home from the optometrist's office a week later, wearing my new horn-rims, each lens about as big around as a thumbnail, I pointed and yelled at everything we passed. I reacted as if no one had seen these things before: billboards, stoplights, other cars, dogs, shrubs. For the first time, the world wasn't an incomprehensible jumble of fuzzy colors without form or purpose. For the first time, the things around me had *edges*.

Not long afterward, we moved to the beige duplex in Green

Bay, Wisconsin. My dad, who had been an in-flight refueler, riding in the belly of KC-135 tankers over Korea and Vietnam, decided to get into recruiting.

We lived on Allouez Avenue, at the bottom of a hill, and most every weeknight I would trudge up that hill to meet my dad on his way home from work. My father was, and is, a bear of a man, and each night when we met, he would reach down with one huge arm and swing me to his shoulders, where I would ride the rest of the trip home, grabbing leaves from the trees we passed to give to my mother. Each night she would thank me, kiss me on the cheek, and put the leaves in a small bud vase over the sink, where they would stay until the next night, when I would give her more.

It was an idyllic, solidly middle-class suburban midwestern childhood.

My dad took me to see awful movies, though we'd never admit how bad they were until we were driving home. He took me to professional wrestling matches, he took me to his office on weekends, to museums, and to see the Packers play. While they had fallen into a slump by the early 1970s, we still went to shiver on the aluminum bleachers of Lambeau Field, happy to be there and at least hope the Pack might come through for us this time. Every once in a while they did.

The Packers, win or lose, defined daily life in Green Bay. Every Sunday during football season, the town shut down completely.

Caught up in the hysteria the way young suburban males will be, I played a lot of football with the neighbor kids in the field behind our small house. It was the best place in the neighborhood to play, so the other kids had to let me join in.

The kids who played came equipped with full uniforms—tiny shoulder pads, padded pants, Packers helmets and jerseys. These were sold as a package deal in sporting goods shops all over town. Officially licensed. As a result, however, everyone who played was number 22. That was the only number printed on jerseys. Things got to be very confusing.

Number 22, it turns out, belonged to a wide receiver named Jon Staggers, who played for the Packers for two seasons. He wasn't the best the franchise had ever seen. Yet because his number appeared on every neighborhood kid's jersey, he received more requests for autographed pictures than anybody else on the team those two seasons.

Maybe it was out of a natural contrariness, maybe it was out of an American love for the underdog, but deep in my heart— hidden, unspoken outside the confines of my own house—I was a Chicago Bears fan. I don't know why. Maybe they just looked tougher. Dick Butkus, their middle linebacker, was a man of primal animal brutality. I admired the way he crushed his opponents, without fear and without mercy.

There was a problem in being a Chicago Bears fan in Green Bay: The Bears and the Packers had been ugly rivals as long as they'd both been around. Whenever they played each other, you knew blood would be spilled.

For my birthday one year, my dad, knowing my affinity for the Bears and wanting to give me something special, called the Chicago home office and ordered me a miniature Dick Butkus uniform. The helmet was black, and the jersey black and red with a big 51 splayed across it. Either my dad wasn't thinking about the trouble this would cause me, or he was looking for a way to toughen me up. I was, after all, a puny and weak child who usually returned home from the sandlot football games in tears.

The first time I proudly donned my new uniform to play with all those number 22s, I had no idea what awaited me. I wasn't trying to antagonize anybody; I simply liked the Bears.

Not only did the rest of the kids refuse to play with me, but cars driving past the field slowed down so the drivers could berate me:

"Traitor!"

"Go back to Russia!"

"Faggot!"

I reckoned that things were getting out of hand when one car screeched onto the sidewalk and stopped. Two men, probably both in their mid-twenties, got out and stomped over to me. Without a word, they pushed me to the ground, got in their car, and squealed away.

I went home after that and vowed never to wear anything but my Bears jersey to these backyard games, and never did. I even took to wearing a Bears hat to Packer games. The other kids eventually let me play with them again. I guess they had to, since it was my backyard.

This was my first experience with what can happen to you if you hold unpopular opinions. It was hardly my last. And in retrospect, these early troubles were mild and innocent.

WITH THE SOLIPSISM OF CHILDHOOD, I figured that as long as I wore my glasses, I was seeing what everyone else could see, and just as well. In sixth grade I started to notice that unless I had a light directly above my chair, it was difficult to read the menu when my parents took me to a restaurant. I resorted to having them order for me rather than admit my failure to see. I didn't know something was wrong, didn't really recognize it as anything serious.

In movie theaters, I was finding it hard, if not impossible, to return to my seat after traipsing into the lobby for another Coke or another box of Chuckles. After a few episodes of wandering up and down the aisle, shouting the name of whoever was there with me, I decided it was better to wait in the lobby until someone came and got me.

Others seemed to stroll about casually in the same light, avoiding furniture and people, reading programs and menus. Ordering their own meals. It took me several years before I saw my predicament in dim light as any sort of a problem.

When I finally recognized my failing eyesight as a problem, I explained my troubles to my optometrist, Dr. Dimlicht. I had been seeing him since we moved to Green Bay.

I dreaded the visits. Seven years I had been going to his office, and never once did he replace the single crummy issue of *Superman* in his waiting room. The other magazines were equally old issues of *Woman's Day* or *Ladies' Home Journal,* one or two of which I was occasionally forced to pick up in desperation. As it turned out, Dr. Dimlicht's wife was my fourth-grade math teacher, the only teacher who ever caught me cheating.

"You try to cheat on any more tests?" he would ask me at each visit as I sat trapped in that big examining chair of his, surrounded by the high-tech gizmos of mid-seventies optometry, no way to escape.

"No, sir," I would always reply meekly.

"That's good, then."

Dr. Dimlicht referred to me as his "star patient," for the sole reason that he'd never had the honor of dealing with someone so young whose eyes were so fucked. When I told him I was having trouble seeing in dark places where other people seemed to function with ease, he excitedly set up a battery of tests. He dilated my pupils, took pictures of the backs of my eyes, tested the pressure inside my eyeballs, everything, jotting down the results in my file as he went along. He even asked about my family's medical history. I knew that one grandmother had cancer and the other had diabetes, but that was about it. I forgot to mention Uncle Tom.

When he had finished the tests, Dr. Dimlicht sat down in his leather chair and looked over his notes. "Well," he began, "it looks like you're night-blind."

That was a disappointment. I knew that much already. I was waiting to hear that I had some fabulously complicated disease. I didn't want to be another "normal" kid. The normal kids would yank my glasses off my face and run up the street, stranding me in the middle of my own backyard with no idea which way they had gone. They always brought the glasses back, sooner or later. Some sooner than others, and always after I had plopped myself down on the ground, sobbing, blind, and hopeless.

Here was my chance to have something to brag about. But no, I was just "night-blind." Dr. Dimlicht didn't mention retinitis pigmentosa. Maybe he thought I wouldn't be able to pronounce it. I left his office that day thinking things were fine except for the fact that I couldn't see at night. When I got home and told my parents, they reacted about the same way I did. Not disappointed the way I had been, but not surprised, either.

At about the same time, the kids in school started spreading rumors. Since I usually stayed away from them, I was prime rumor material. Most of the rumors, stories about my parents or my sexual preference, came and went in a few days, but one of these rumors wouldn't go away. Though nobody came right out and asked me, I heard things.

"Jim's reading all the time because he's going blind. He's trying to cram as much as possible into his head before he does."

This rumor persisted, year after year, until I graduated from high school. It followed me through three different schools and several turnovers in the student body.

At the time, I had no idea that I really *was* going blind. I knew my vision was bad, yet since I lived with it on a daily basis, it seemed reasonably stable. If Dr. Dimlicht had explained retinitis pigmentosa to me, if he had taken his time, gone through it slowly, I might have had some clue as to what was facing me.

If I had known what lay ahead I would have done more than waste all those years of childhood assuming there was still a lifetime left to, well, look at things. But I thought that as long as I kept my glasses on, or bought all the snacks I needed before the movie started, I'd be fine.

THE SUMMER I TURNED FOURTEEN, my sister was studying to get her degree in special education from the University of Wisconsin at Oshkosh. As part of her field training, Mary elected to take part in a local program called Respite, in which presumably "normal" families took in mentally retarded and emotionally disturbed kids for a few weeks. It gave the kids' parents a break, a chance to catch their breath, maybe take a regular vacation.

Mary discussed the program with my parents, got their approval, and started making preparations weeks in advance. Somehow, though, no one bothered to tell me about all this, let alone ask my opinion.

David showed up on a Saturday morning in early June. He had Down's syndrome and the physical problems that came with it—ears that needed draining, a weakened heart, and retardation. He arrived also with the energy of an eight-year-old and the bad attitude of a child who had been abandoned by his mother. She never got out of her car; just chatted with my sister and parents briefly through the window, then backed out of the driveway and sped off to Florida.

We brought David in and showed him around. He was to have my room, I was informed, and I would sleep on a couch in the basement. That was fine, I figured. It would be like camping out.

After an hour of getting acquainted—the rest of the family charmed to death by this bundle of energy, me still astonished by the strange twist my summer had taken—my dad suggested I take David to the backyard, play baseball with him or something.

I grabbed a Wiffle ball and bat from the garage, and led him outside. I handed the bat to our houseguest and turned to walk a few feet away to pitch the ball to him. Before I had taken two steps, though, he was on me, swinging the bat as hard as he could against my lower back, then my legs, then my arms.

Gonna be a hell of a summer, I thought as I yanked the bat out of his hands, grateful that I'd decided not to go with the aluminum one.

And indeed, a strange and savage dichotomy revealed itself. Whenever my parents and sister were around, David was the sweetest boy on earth. A child who had been dealt a bad hand yet had a glowing, warm heart of gold despite it all. But when they left, when it was the two of us alone together, that heart of gold froze into lead, and he would attack me with whatever weapons might be handy. Or he would try to kill the cat or smash the aquarium.

When I brought this up with my parents, they gave me that hard "Don't be jealous" look and dismissed my concern. I wanted to show them the bruises on my legs, the scratches on my arms, but was stopped before I had the chance.

After a few days of everyone's staying around to help ease

David's transition, things got back to normal. What that meant was that both my folks went back to work, and my sister began work as a counselor at a five-day-a-week camp for "special kids." That left me home alone with Satan's Own Mistake eight to ten hours a day. The moment the door closed for the last time in the morning, with my sister leaving about nine, the war began. David usually started off by spitting at me, then swept whatever was on the nearest table onto the floor, then took off after the cat. I never should have shown him where I kept the Wiffle bat. The mayhem continued nonstop until he heard a car pull into the driveway in the evening. Then he'd stop, his smile would return, and he'd greet whoever came in the front door with hugs and sweet little kisses.

If I wasn't sweeping broken glass off the floor or picking it out of my body, my parents often found me in the basement, shaking, exhausted, almost unable to speak.

"What's wrong with you?" they'd ask.

"He's evil," I'd tell them.

"He's *evil*, now? I think you're a young man who has to learn a little bit about maturity," my dad would say. "You've got to remember that he has special problems, he's not as smart or as old as you are."

"Fine," I'd reply, knowing that if you didn't see the way David went for that knife drawer, you would never understand.

Day after day this went on. On the weekends, when the rest of the family was home, I couldn't even hide in my room and lock the door and let everyone else deal with him, because it was his room now. On the weekends I took a lot of long walks and went to see a lot of movies, again and again.

At the beginning of the second week, I started fighting back. I never laid a hand on him, except to remove the Wiffle bat or to pry his stubby claws from around the cat's throat. Instead, I got him where I knew it would really hurt.

"Chewie's *dead*." I'd hiss at him flatly. "Darth Vader chopped him into bite-sized pieces and *ate* him."

"*Chewie! Chewie noooo!*" he'd scream, before burying his face in his hands and dropping to the floor like a small pile of fleshy laundry.

That'll keep him going for a while, I thought smugly to myself. David was a huge *Star Wars* fanatic. It was nearly all he thought about when he wasn't plotting my demise. Chewbacca was his favorite.

My real revenge came one Sunday when my mom and dad were out and I went to see some movie three times in a row. That left my sister—the one who had gotten me into this predicament in the first place, the one who wanted to do this for the rest of her life—alone with David for eight hours. When my parents and I got back home, she was in tears, and David was all smiles and kisses.

"I had no idea what it would be like," she said, "to be alone with him for a whole day. He's a little monster."

I didn't say anything. I went and turned on the television, wondering if my parents were giving her the quiet "maturity" speech.

When David's mother came to pick him up, looking tanned but no less haggard, she still didn't get out of the car. She opened the passenger door and let him crawl in. After the rest of my family said their tearful good-byes, I strolled up to his window. I figured it would be a nice gesture, a minor act for my parents' sake, a cheap scheme to avoid another lecture once he was gone for good.

David leaned out of his window in an effort, it appeared, to give me a kiss. I leaned in close, trying to hide my grimace at the prospect of carrying out this lie to such a degree, and he

spit in my face. Then he rolled up his window and they drove
away.

DESPITE A LOVING FAMILY and a stable home life, as I
entered my middle teens things started to go very wrong. Not
just with my eyes, which were noticeably worse, but inside my
head as well. I became a grim and lonely youth, who spoke little
and had few friends. I crashed headlong into a serious case of
annoying adolescent angst, burying myself in Nietzsche, Camus,
and Sartre, filling notebooks with maudlin and self-pitying prose,
casually inflicting pain upon myself, picking fights—physical
and philosophical—that I knew I could never win. I was discov-
ering that people were much more interesting and attractive
before they opened their mouths. Once they spoke, all such
illusions of beauty, charisma, and intelligence vanished. I
became filled with the contempt and hatred for the world and
humanity so common among bright young boys who read too
much and listen to punk rock.

Unlike most cases of stereotypical teen angst, however, this
dose wouldn't pass for a while.

Even with my moods and my wallowing, my anger and my
self-pity, there were still a few friends in high school who put up
with me. There was Peter. And Paul and Ellen and Steve.

Peter, while he looked like me—same glasses, same hair-
cut—was harder, more athletic, more conniving and militant.
He tried to model himself after Cassius in *Julius Caesar.* Paul
was an obsessive about everything he came in contact with:
Pepsi, Pat Benatar, politics. Ellen had had a rough time of it—
bad crowd, bad attitude. She was hefty, but in a cute way. She
wanted to clean up her act and felt Peter, Paul, Steve, and I were
nerdy enough to help her do that. Then there was Steve. Steve

was soft and spoke with a lilting lisp. The son of a philosophy professor, he collected textbooks and had, in the confines of his room, the largest collection of Abba recordings in the world. It was Steve who, three years later, would walk me to the hospital after I cut my wrists.

We had gravitated toward one another accidentally in the halls of East High, each of us an outcast for our own reasons, each of us freaks in our own way. That was enough of a glue to hold us together. We were all smart, but not as smart as we thought we were. We all had a healthy taste for the absurd. Whatever we did we ended up doing together.

There wasn't much to do in Green Bay during the summer, and the summer after we graduated we were especially bored. We had seen every movie we wanted to see. No bands came to town that we could agree on seeing. None of us drank, so that was out. Peter had a fancy swimming pool at his house, but he never invited us to use it. Mostly we just drove around, listened to the radio, and laughed at things. That was usually enough, but not one July afternoon. We were crammed into Paul's car: Steve, Peter, Ellen, Paul, of course, who was driving, and I.

"There's always the sanitarium," I suggested, while Steve desperately spun the radio dial, trying to find something he liked.

"Again with the sanitarium," Paul grumbled dismissively. I was always suggesting the sanitarium.

"Something to do."

The sanitarium, sitting in the dry, dead country on the outskirts of DePere, a fifteen-minute drive away, was the local haunted house. We had heard legends about it since we were kids, but had never been there. Sneaking in was a local teenage rite of passage.

The sanitarium opened in the forties as a hospital where locals with tuberculosis were quarantined. In the fifties, it admitted anyone with any dread infectious disease, anything that threatened an epidemic—whooping cough and the like. Then, in the sixties, it was turned into a madhouse. This is all very well documented. Legends sprouted about what, exactly, went on at the hospital. When the place shut down in 1969 (rumor has it, in order to cover up a series of axe-murders that had occurred there), it became an immediate destination for bored teenagers looking for cheap thrills. It was also perfect for beer parties.

The crazy axe-murderer still lived there, naturally, and chopped up anyone he caught sneaking in. This story expanded into a number of clues and further myths. If the front door was open, the murderer was out. If the light over the garage door was on, he was home. Four kids had disappeared there *just three years ago* (it was always "three years ago"). I was never sure whether or not my sister went out there, but she certainly knew all about it. Something in my head and guts told me that I had to go and see it for myself. Unfortunately, none of my friends was quite as excited about the sanitarium as I was.

"Go out there and get chopped up? I don't think so," Steve said, after settling on some pop song on the radio.

"We're not gonna get chopped up. I just want to see what it's like."

"Why?"

"I'm curious. What else are we doing?"

After a few more minutes of encouragement and whining on my part, the other four agreed. It was six o'clock, there was plenty of time left to find the sanitarium, get in, look around, and get out while it was still light.

Given, that is, that we weren't murdered by an axe-wielding maniac.

We stopped at Steve's house to pick up flashlights, and while we were there, I called my sister for directions.

"Take that road west out of DePere, you know the one. It'll take about ten minutes. It'll be on the right, you can't miss it." She sounded surprised that her pale, skinny twist of a brother was making the trip.

We crawled back into Paul's car and headed over the bridge into DePere, a brown little industrial suburb, found the road she had told me about, and headed west, where the buildings gave way to farmland and sparse woods.

Odd thing was, just as everyone else in the car was getting more excited, I, having made the perhaps fatal decision, was getting more frightened. I didn't believe the legends; I was smarter than that. But something prickly and sinister was bothering me. It was too late to suggest we turn around, to convince them I had been kidding, trying to see if they'd fall for such a stupid idea. I couldn't do that. I was in it now, and I was scared. I just stared out the window and waited.

About a quarter-mile past a ramshackle wooden church, we saw it. Gray towers rose above a dense thicket of dying trees. It was bigger than I had expected. A dead fortress of thick stone walls and broken windows, in the middle of nowhere, like some vampire's castle.

Paul slowed down and pulled over to the side of the road. We stared at our intended destination.

"So how are we gonna do this?"

I was vaguely hoping nobody would be able to come up with a plan, that we would settle for seeing the place and then go home.

"We park the car here, and any cops come by, they'll know exactly what's going on," Peter said. "This is still trespassing, so what we do is this. . . ." Damn that Peter. He was the strategist of the bunch. Had a plan for everything. "We go back to that church and park there. Then we circle around and come in the back way. There's gotta be a way in there—all the windows have been smashed in."

I couldn't help noticing, as we sat there, that the light above the garage door was on. I didn't point it out.

Paul turned the car around and headed toward the church. We had passed only one or two cars on the way out, which was good, I suppose. Fewer witnesses. He pulled the car behind some trees off the church's tiny gravel parking lot, and we got out.

The church, long abandoned too, had itself become part of the legend. It was where the guy with the axe held his satanic masses. We peeked through the windows. No butchered goats, no bloodstains, no pentagrams.

Flashlights in hand, we walked around the back of the church and into the field that separated us from the sanitarium. The grass was waist-high, and as we slowly marched through it, I kept my eyes down, pointlessly looking for muskrat traps. There were none, of course; we were a few miles from any river, but I was sure I was going to step into a trap and lose a foot.

After carefully climbing through a homemade barbed-wire fence, we saw that getting in wasn't going to be a problem. The back door had been ripped off its hinges.

"Well," I asked, as we stood there, "who's gonna go first?"

"Well, that's pretty simple," Ellen said. "This was *your* stupid idea."

The rest of them grunted and chuckled in agreement. I was now hoping we would run into the guy with the axe. I took a flashlight from Steve and switched it on. I'm not sure why, because flashlights had never done me a damn bit of good, except for close jobs. They never ended up working quite as well as they did in the movies.

I stepped through the door, with the others crowding behind me. I could barely see a thing. The floor was crunchy with broken plaster and shards of glass, and littered with beer cans.

We split up and started exploring. Steve and Ellen came with me. We found a staircase that seemed solid, and went upstairs. On the first landing, I shined the light on the walls. Someone had scrawled "He's coming for your ass!" on one wall. That alone might have been almost disturbing, except that the same person had scrawled "Twisted Sister" beneath it, and "666" next to that with the same marker.

"Oooh, scary." Steve smirked. We continued to the second floor.

The second floor had evidently been some sort of ward. There were no doors left, so we peeked into each of the dozen grimy concrete-walled rooms we came to, hoping to find something interesting. Only more plaster, more beer cans and cigarette butts.

In one room, bunched up in the middle of the floor, was a tatter of brown shag carpeting. It was the only decoration left.

"Imagine how many diseases it holds," I said, after Steve suggested that we might take the rug home with us.

A car passed by outside, headlights flashing through the broken windows. It slowed down, and I snapped the flashlight off. I snapped it back on when the car drove away.

The sanitarium was, on the whole, surprisingly boring. Empty rooms, beer cans, and filth. We went downstairs and met up with Peter and Paul, who had found more of the same.

"Well, at least we did it. That's something," I said. Nobody seemed too disappointed that we had made the trip, or that we hadn't found a single dismembered body.

Just as we were deciding to go, Paul noticed a flight of stairs leading down. "Wait, we *have* to check out the basement," he said.

I was ready to leave, and was beginning to worry about whether I might have caught TB from that carpet upstairs. "You go check out the basement. If you find anything interesting, give us a shout."

He took the steps gingerly downward and disappeared into the gloom. A minute later, he was back.

"There's all this furniture scattered around, like chairs and couches, but it's all flooded, everything's half underwater. And it smells really bad."

"I guess we don't have to go see it, then," I said.

We walked out the way we had come in, but instead of sneaking to the church through the field, we went to the front of the sanitarium, through the trees, and out to the two-lane highway in front. We strolled down the road in rough single file, brazenly swinging our flashlights at our sides. If people saw us now, they'd know exactly where we had been. Well, fuck 'em. We had done it. We had taken the plunge, no matter how pointless and boring a plunge it might ultimately have been. We had confronted the local myth and come away alive.

We got into Paul's car, sweaty and quietly pleased with ourselves, and drove back to town. It didn't occur to me until years later why I had wanted to break into the sanitarium so badly in the first place, and why I wanted to run when the opportunity finally arose. It only made sense that something deep inside my brain, some genetic prescience, knew that I would be spending so much time in real madhouses later.

s l a c k j a w

ONE EVENING after Latin class, my friend Grinch and I sat in my cramped apartment passing a bottle of wine back and forth, smoking bad cigars, playing the easy-listening station on the radio. Even though we were hard-core—we looked the part and went to the shows—we found it absurd, ridiculous, and very punk rock to tune in easy-listening music while surrounded by squalor. It was a contradiction that made perfect sense to us, especially so close to what we hoped would be the final days of Western Civilization. I was lost in the 101 Strings' rendition of "Raindrops Keep Fallin' on My Head," when Grinch said:

"We should start a political party."

He and I had met in a course entitled "Violence and Catharsis." We were both philosophy majors. We were in the same Dostoevsky class. Same Kafka and Latin classes as well. We were in a lot of classes together. It was inevitable that we started talking.

Grinch was full of tales of a misspent youth. He had done the drugs and the petty crimes, he had been in fights, he had been punk rock before anyone knew what punk rock was, and he had done a stint in the Army before being discharged for an "extremely poor attitude."

At first, I didn't believe his stories. We were two guys sitting around telling lies to each other, the way guys do. Grinch was doing his best to shock me. I had never done drugs, and never drank much. I'd never stolen so much as a piece of candy or a comic book. Never smoked a cigarette. I'd been a good kid, or tried to be. I was still a simple midwestern boy, curious and confused about what was going on in my head.

It was only a week after I walked out of that shrink's office and smashed those windows that Grinch showed up, as if delivered postage-due by Satan himself. Grinch was smart and borderline psychotic. He was sociopathic at the least. Everybody seemed to know Grinch. He was tall, wiry, and a few years older than most of the other undergrads. He had a quavery drawl that the Army had given him, curly black hair, and the sharp good looks that drew college girls to him at the snap of his fingers.

He snapped his fingers a lot, and I always had the good sense to excuse myself. The girls never found out how diabolical he was until it was too late. But even then they usually didn't care. They kept coming back.

It all started so simply in its own way. I was a beginner. Grinch showed me how to steal, drink, and smoke. He taught me the proper method for breaking into a building after hours—which never did me a whole lot of good, because I could never see anything once I got inside. He showed me the cheap and useless joys of vandalism.

Early on, we prided ourselves on being political. We went to all the protest rallies and all the marches, we helped build shantytowns to protest apartheid and once, with several hundred members of the Progressive Student Network, took over the State Capitol for two weeks. In the fall we would join activists and protest the CIA's recruiting on campus, and in the spring we'd protest the university's South African investments. After a while, though, we grew bored with the political thing, the same faces, the same tired chants. We realized we didn't like the people we were protesting with any more than we liked the people we were protesting against.

The breaking point came during a protest against South African investments. I was marching down State Street toward the Capitol with two thousand true believers chanting and carrying signs. I had been hornswoggled into helping carry a banner near the front of the mob. I had no idea what it said. Nevertheless, being on the front lines gave me the privilege of conducting chants of my own, I figured.

"The time! Has come! To wipe out fascist scum!" I yelled, hoping others would join in. A few people around me tittered nervously, but I was alone in my zeal.

An aging earth mother to my right turned to me. "Fascists are scary, yes," she said, in a tone far too condescending for my taste, "but that's no reason to threaten them with violence." Oh, Jesus. I handed her my end of the banner and went home.

Now, as we shared that bottle of cheap wine in my tiny, ant-ridden apartment, Grinch's suggestion didn't surprise me. Little of what Grinch said surprised me anymore.

"Think about it. We spend our nights now running around Madison doing all this shit. We form a political party, and we have an excuse. It's a fuckin' umbrella excuse for *everything*. We get recognition from the university as some kind of student organization and that gets us access to even more shit."

"Like what?"

Grinch appeared to have thought this whole thing through. He looked down at the bottle. "Well, all kinds of shit. We'll find that out later."

Maybe he'd thought it through only halfway, but it was more than I had to offer.

"What the hell," I responded, and took the bottle from him.

"First thing we need is a name. Something that will confuse people."

We sat in silence for a minute.

" 'Pharmacists for Change'?" I offered.

"No, no."

We paused and thought again.

" 'Necrophiles for Change'?" I offered next.

"Better, but too obvious."

After a few more rounds, Grinch came up with "Nihilist Workers' Party." As philosophy majors, we had a bad habit of overexplaining things to each other.

"The joke is"—Grinch laughed—"if we were nihilists, why would we work? And moreover, why would we ever form a political party?"

There we were. The party was born, and we couldn't wait to make our first appearance the next day. I went into my closet, where I had some immense sheets of cardboard stashed, waiting for an opportunity like this.

The University of Wisconsin's student union was a huge, rambling building on the shores of Lake Mendota. Various additions to the building had made it into an architectural muddle of five or six dramatically different styles spread along a city block. Just inside was a lobby, with a café to the right and bulletin boards announcing meetings scheduled in the union that week. Down the hall to the left was the Rathskeller, where underage students drank for cheap.

On weekdays the lobby was lined with folding tables manned by students in organizations vying for new recruits: Socialists, ROTC, NOW, Young Republicans, Revolutionary Communists, the student paper.

I got to the union early, grabbed the table closest to the door, and set up shop. I put out the obligatory donations jar, taped the requisite petition on the table, and hung up our sign, which read, in a thick Magic Marker scrawl, "The Nihilist Workers' Party Says, If You Think Education Is Expensive, Try Ignorane." We only half intentionally misspelled "ignorance." Fact was, we ran out of room on the poster.

From my bag I pulled out a small but representative sample of the ignorance we had encountered in the world. Religious pamphlets, pages from nineteenth-century physics textbooks, Catholic marriage manuals, ill-conceived political screeds. Our concept was simple: A four-year university education cost thousands upon thousands of dollars, but the caring folks of the NWP were willing to sell to anyone who was interested a lifetime's worth of ignorance for a mere quarter.

I managed to sell ignorance to only one befuddled old man before a hippie woman with long straight hair, big round glasses, and a black turtleneck threw me out. To commandeer a table, as it happened, I had to belong to a recognized student organization and had to reserve the table weeks in advance. Grinch and I discussed a new strategy.

At eight o'clock the next morning, I returned with him. Getting there early, we were guaranteed a free table until the legitimate organization that had signed up for it arrived. This time, we were there to conduct the official NWP Bake Sale. We had stopped at a grocery store and loaded up on an array of Hostess products, and had made a tape loop of me reading the ingredients of a Twinkie. We didn't sell anything before we were thrown out again, by the same woman.

We returned every morning for the rest of the week, each morning with a new ploy, and every morning we would be thrown out within half an hour. We simply refused to take the hint.

FROM THE BACK of an anarchist book catalogue, I made a hundred photocopies of a list of toll-free numbers of organiza-

tions, including the Moral Majority, nuclear weapons manufac-
turers, and Dow Chemical. Our plan was basic telephone terrorism. Every call made to a toll-free number costs the people
who pick up the phone money. The longer you talk, the more it
costs them. We didn't care who was on that list, as long as we were
fucking things up for somebody. We put fliers—the photocopied
lists, with instructions—on the table and sat there. They were
gone before we were ousted.

Afterward we wandered around Madison to see what other
trouble we might cause, and I forgot about the fliers. Until the
next day, when I picked up the student newspaper.

Our flier had been reprinted, word for word, on the editor-
ial page. What's more, the paper had credited the NWP with a
byline. Grinch and I got to thinking. The people at the paper had
given us a byline. That meant they wanted us to write for them.
This was their quiet way of offering us a regular column. I sat
down at my blue plastic Smith-Corona, fired up a nasty cigar, and
wrote our first.

HOW TO BUILD A CHEAP BOMB

Don't you all agree—ah, you all must agree —that there
comes a time in everyone's life when we all want to be Elvis,
when we all want to be Joan of Arc, we all want to be Jerry
Lewis, we all want to be Jeane Kirkpatrick, or Golda Meir,
or John Stuart Mill, or Jackie Gleason, or Jocko the Apeshit
Boy, or Veebo the Born Philosopher, or Bozo the Evil, Axe
Wielding Clown, or a large bottle of Top Job, or some de-
hydrated tomatoes, or a brainwave, or some Silly Putty, or
some Schmaltz E Dige artificial chicken-flavored fat, or a
squashed toad, or Samuel J. Mecklenburg, or Jesse James,

or Fatty Arbuckle, or *any* Arbuckle, or Elvis again, or an Elvis impersonator, or an Elvis-impersonator impersonator, or a prayer rug, or a black velvet painting, or a militant plumber, or a pen scratch, or a hang-gliding gnu, or some hooves, or a set of nontoxic watercolor paints, or one quarter of a horse, or some mildewed peaches, or glumness, or a book bindery, or Gumby's tiny brown muscular alien friend, Mike, or Archie and Marlene of the Nashville North Show Lounge, or matzoh, or a famous composer of commercial jingles, or Kirk Douglas, or a thin line of spittle hanging from someone's lower lip, or a dent, or nostrils, or maybe even a creature once thought extinct like the coelacanth except not a fish but something much larger and not so slimy, or one of the Osmond clan, or a puddle, or a waste dump, or a dental hygienist, or dialectical materialism, or the categorical imperative, or the reason why a hammer is *not* a plaything, or the phrase "Moms like it, too!" or Aunt Jemima, or the jitterbug, or a cricket nailed to a piece of corkboard, or some old dead guy nobody liked, or Betsy the Boilsucker, or hair, or a mile of unpaved road, or "that funky disco beat," or some convulsions.

Am I right? So be careful, dammit, and don't blow off any fingers.

It took me fifteen minutes of hard labor to churn that out, hard labor that went unrecognized, since *The Daily Cardinal* refused to print it, too busy as it was documenting atrocities taking place in Nicaragua or South Africa or El Salvador. Two days after breaking into the *Cardinal*'s offices to leave our first brilliant foray into journalism on the editor's desk, we stopped by during business hours to find out why it hadn't run yet.

The editor's name was Marcia. She was a chain-smoker

with long straight hair, heavy bags under her eyes, and a well-cultivated world-weariness about her.

"Guys," she told us, patient as could be, gesturing to the poorly typed manuscript on her desk. "Let's be realistic. This doesn't make any sense."

"Makes sense to me," I said.

"Absolutely crystalline," Grinch added.

We were very serious.

"Guys, c'mon. Everyone wants to be Elvis? What the hell does that mean?"

Grinch and I looked at each other. Now *she* was the one who wasn't making any sense.

"I wanna be Elvis," Grinch said.

"Me, too," I added. "No question, I wanna be Elvis."

"I can name several professors who want to be Elvis."

"And frankly, Marcia, I'm worried about the fact that you *don't* want to be Elvis."

We were quietly ushered from the office and asked never to return.

Two weeks later we began to notice the fallout from our telephone terrorism stunt. A local right-wing magazine named us "Jerks of the Month" and claimed we were being investigated by the FBI. Radio call-in shows were abuzz with voices spouting theory after theory about who or what this Nihilist Workers' Party was all about. Most people thought we were government spies attempting to discredit the left, but that was typical for Madison. There was even a mention in *Time* magazine, under the headline "Toll-Free Woes." After our flier was reprinted in the student paper, *Time* reported, organizations on the list received as many as fifteen hundred calls a day from the Madison area. Especially Jerry Falwell. Nobody liked him.

We had done our job well, except for one minor detail: a

Supreme Court decision passed the year before had ruled that telephone terrorism constituted a federal offense. Our names had not appeared in the paper, only the name of our "organization." While the feds questioned university officials and the editors of the *Cardinal,* we skipped away. They were the ones who had decided to print it; we had never even pitched it to the paper as a good idea. We were nothing but innocent bystanders. Even if the feds did trace it back to us, they would have to go one step further, to the folks who put out that anarchist book catalogue.

We never worried about that supposed FBI investigation, anyway. What was there to uncover about us? Tap our phones and there'd be two guys ranting and raving and laughing about nothing. With the student union and the newspaper off-limits, we had to find something else to keep us occupied.

IN THE MIDST of the mayhem, I graduated with a degree in philosophy and started looking for grad schools. I had another nine months before I would be moving to . . . well, wherever. I decided to stay in Madison and hunt for a job, and continued living in that treacherous apartment. Grinch and I ran wild in the streets, tormenting political candidates, getting thrown out of coffeehouses and beat up at punk shows, stealing books, interrupting performance artists, vandalizing whatever we could, beating up Moonies, drinking beer, and hosting parades—all in the name of the Nihilist Workers' Party, just so it would mean something.

One night not long after graduation, Grinch and I were in the Rathskeller. It was nearly closing time, and the place had cleared out. Grinch went to get another pitcher while I sat at the table, chewing on stale popcorn and programming horrid songs on the jukebox behind me.

I was maybe three or four beers over the line and exhausted, and didn't want to talk anymore. I didn't want to think anymore. I just wanted to go back to my room to get some sleep so I could get up the next day and spend the first four hours recovering so we could do the same thing the next night.

When I got into this state, whether from drinking or reading Aristotle, my mouth tended to drop open. And there it would stay—it took too much energy to close it.

It happened while I was waiting for Grinch to return with the pitcher that would make my recovery the next day only slower and more painful. He came up from behind me, set the plastic pitcher down on the scarred wooden table, and clopped me under the jaw with his free hand.

"Hey, *slackjaw*. Wake up!"

I glared at him as I rubbed my chin and felt around the inside of my mouth with my tongue to make sure I hadn't chipped any more teeth.

"Slackjaw, huh?" I finally said. I had heard the name before, but never applied to me. Usually we cast it at the mumblers and screamers who cornered us at bus stops.

"Grinch and Slackjaw," he said, satisfied, pouring himself a beer. "Sounds like a match made in hell."

"Comic-book hell, maybe."

a real american

I WAS AN IMMIGRANT fresh off the boat. I had a degree I could not use from a university I did not care about in a town I wanted to burn to the ground. No job to take up my time and no money to worry about. The mattress on my floor had become home to millions of black wood ants. For the most part I spent my days reading, wandering around, drinking bottle after bottle of vile, sweet homemade cherry wine, causing trouble with Grinch—who still had course work to worry about—and squeezing ants, one after another, between my fingers.

It was clear that I had to do something more. I had to make money, if only to keep the apartment. The rent was $185 a month, which was $185 a month more than I had coming in.

For other kids, it seemed, it was easy. Just call up the folks and wait for the check. I was hiding from my parents the depths to which I had sunk, and keeping my destitution to myself, holding my head as high as I could. Whenever I did speak to them I did my best to convince them that everything was "just fine."

I looked in the classifieds day after day for work, but nobody was advertising for a "philosopher-bum w/keen sense of absurd." I wasn't particularly interested in working, anyway. I was happy enough with my foul cherry wine and my ants. There had to be another way. There is always another way to do everything.

I picked up a newspaper while strolling around one morning, and sat down on a park bench to read it. An ad at the bottom of one page caught my eye.

It was an ad for one of those plasma centers, like the Red Cross, but more profitable. You won't find altruistic citizens giving the gift of life at a plasma center. The people who come to a plasma center are there because they need the twenty-five bucks a week that's offered in exchange for their precious bodily fluid. The Desperate, I believe we call them in America.

I found a pay phone on the corner outside the center and made an appointment for that afternoon. When I entered, the place was packed to overflowing with philosopher-bums, most of whom I knew from around town. There was Rat-Faced Earl, with his long yellow teeth, matted beard, plaid shirt, and copy of *Atlas Shrugged*. Beside him was his eternal silent shadow, Edward. And there was Crazy Jake, whom I had often seen standing outside B-Side Records, shrieking. Dunderhead and Lummox were there, too, another team. One by one our names were announced, and we were led into a back room by a nurse.

When I was summoned, I was led through a room with three desks, each with a dumpy nurse siphoning blood out of someone, and into a small room where a doctor who had apparently failed in some terrible way was sitting in a chair behind a bare desk. A clock on the wall and a molded plastic chair for me provided the remaining decor. The doctor pulled a sheet of paper out of his desk drawer and handed it to me with undisguised contempt.

"Here. Read this."

I did. It was a fact sheet on AIDS. By this time, 1985, with news about AIDS filtering down to the public, people in the blood-for-sale industry suspected what they were up against, and they were doing their best to keep their asses covered.

I scanned it and handed it back.

"Now I'm going to give you a quiz on what you just read."

"Aww, Jesus, fuck."

"You take the quiz or you can leave." He didn't want to be

there, and I didn't want to be there with him, but I needed that twenty-five bucks.

He asked me his little questions, and I shot back my little answers, and after I had gotten enough right to satisfy him, he sent me off to a nurse, who pulled out another set of questions.

"Did you eat a good breakfast?"

"Yes." (Pringles and a glass of water was a decent meal for me at the time.)

"In the past week, have you had any unexplained night sweats?"

"No."

"Unexplained fever?"

"No."

"Unexplained weight loss?"

"No."

A litany of potential symptoms of one blood disease or another she shot at me, almost all of which demanded a no if I wanted to stick around any longer. An occasional yes question was thrown in to trip up the unwary, but I was careful, and before long the nurse was tying a rubber tube around my arm.

She pricked my finger with a lancet, and while I was signing a variety of consent and "Yes, I am telling the truth" forms, she put a drop of my blood into a machine that whipped it around at ultrasonic speed to separate the platelets from the plasma, to see if there was enough iron to deem my juice that day as salable.

Having passed that test, I was pointed to the Bleeding Room, as I came to know it, where another nurse led me to the nearest empty dentist's chair and strapped me in. There were thirty chairs, each surrounded by a tangle of primitive blood-sucking equipment.

Another apparently failed doctor, a young, short, hip-looking guy who had penance to do, was running from chair to chair, sticking needles in people, checking bags, telling jokes, making cheap passes at the nurses while elbowing the bums with a sly wink. You could tell that nobody was screwing anybody there.

Eventually he got around to me, made a few cursory introductory remarks, and set to fumbling with the equipment. The process, in theory, was simple: suck two bags of blood out of your arm, spin them around a while, skim the plasma off the top, and shoot the red blood cells right back into you. But the tangle of tubes and needles and bags was inevitably messed up in some way, and usually one unconnected tube spewed precious red fluid on the dirty gray floor.

I got paid only ten dollars for my first visit. That was the scam. To make the full twenty-five, I had to come a second time the same week, when I would be paid the balance.

That left me making twenty-five dollars a week, a hundred a month. Still not enough to pay the rent. I took another look in the paper and found several plasma centers in the region, all independent. I tracked down Rat Face and he told me that a few of the centers didn't check donor lists against one another's. After scheduling myself at the first place for Tuesdays and Fridays, I went to a second place and went through exactly the same procedure. Same failed doctors, same dumpy nurses, same philosopher-bums. There I set up a Monday/Thursday schedule. Then I went to the last place (the difference here was that the nurses were slightly better-looking and more incompetent) and scheduled myself for Wednesdays and Saturdays.

In a week I went from making nothing to making $300 a month, enough to cover rent and utilities with some left over for occasionally decent groceries. Beer in bottles, even. Only problem was, I was being sucked dry. After a few weeks, I was sleeping until half an hour before my appointments, then coming straight home to sleep again. My movements, never exactly lightning-quick to begin with, slowed down. I killed just those ants on my mattress that crawled over my body. My pale face became almost luminous.

Bill Burroughs wrote, "If after having been exposed to someone's presence, you feel as if you've lost a quart of plasma, *avoid* that presence."

That kept running through my head while I was strapped down in the centers, unable to think clearly of anything else. I repeated it in my mind as Rat-Faced Earl, in the next chair, talked to me about objectivism. I repeated it as the nurses dropped my blood bags. I repeated it and repeated it, but I never heeded it, and I slowly let the vampires kill me.

I would pull the cotton swab off my arm the moment I stepped out of the centers, and let the fresh, whole, thick blood run down my arm and pool in my cupped hand. I started to look like the junkies who clustered in Madison's Peace Park. In a way, I had become one, only in reverse. Instead of paying someone to give me something to shoot into my veins, I was being paid to let someone suck something out. I was just as hooked. And the culture was much the same. Instead of shooting galleries, we had sucking galleries. And our pushers kept offering us more money if we kept returning. I even grew to love the needle more than the payoff, the way the hard-core junkies do. It was an enormous needle, too, and in that initial puncture, watching it slide under the skin, the bulge in the arm, the first blast of blood through the clear tubes, I had found another kind of happiness.

Fortunately, and by accident, a porn shop hired me as a clerk some weeks after I had become seriously hooked into the plasma centers. Things started looking up for a while.

I MET GRINCH ONE NIGHT at his apartment. He lived in a foul, humid, roach-infested few rooms with two Vietnamese students who spoke no English. The place always stank of rotting fish. It wasn't exactly pleasant to visit, and it was a relief to get out of there.

We didn't have any plans for the night. We never did. If nothing happened, we made something happen and then sat back and watched the results. Sometimes Grinch would put on a pair of handcuffs and run down the street while I chased him (making sure never to get close enough to grab him), screaming, "Stop him! Somebody stop him!" to see what people would do.

Maybe tonight we'd check out O'Cayz Corral, the local punk club, to see who was playing. Come nine-thirty, we decided to head out. As we approached the campus, we continued the animated discussion we'd started in Grinch's kitchen.

All of a sudden my ears started ringing. What's more, the perspective of my vision shifted. Now, instead of looking up the street, I was looking up at the sky. Or more precisely, up at Grinch's face staring down at me, saying something I couldn't make out. My left ear was numb. There was a strange sensation in my head, almost pain, but not quite. It felt like something that would be pain very soon, though.

I was lying on my back, on the sidewalk.

"Didn't you see that pole?" Grinch's twang ripped through the air. "Hey, Slack—didn't you see that fucking pole?" As long as we had known each other, I had had to keep reminding Grinch that my eyes were bad, that I couldn't see too well at night. He kept forgetting. Sometimes so did I.

I looked around, my eyes not focusing on much until they zeroed in on the streetlamp twenty feet above me, jutting out from a black steel pole, nearly a foot in diameter, which rose from the sidewalk. A pole that was still quivering and ringing itself, apparently from the high-speed impact of my skull.

"Christ, we were walking along, talking," Grinch went on, frightened and excited. "I figured you saw it, then boom! Y'know? *Boom!* Down you went." He started laughing, and laughing hysterically. And I started laughing, too, if only because I always laugh, or smile nervously, in situations like this.

"You're all three fuckin' Stooges rolled into one!" he choked out.

I raised my arm for Grinch to help me up, then made a gesture for my hat, which he retrieved and jammed, crooked, on my head.

"Boy." My legs rickety, I leaned against the assailant pole for support. "Boy oh boy." It was taking some effort to get my tongue moving the way I wanted it to, and Grinch stood there staring at me. "Boy oh boy. Did not see that coming at all." I laughed again, more fragile this time. "Y'know . . . Grinch?" I spoke carefully, testing the words before I spoke them. "Y'know . . . I think I . . . should probably head back home. I'm, uhh . . . I'm not feeling too swell."

It wasn't that my head hurt. It didn't. My stomach had cramped up on me, and I felt like I was going to puke. I still couldn't feel my left ear, or hear much of anything with it. My knees were threatening to buckle again.

"Sure," Grinch said. "You need any help? You gonna be able to get back there all right?"

I took inventory. I was standing, I was speaking, I knew what had happened. I had slammed the left side of my skull into a steel lamppost while walking along at a nice clip. Now I was loopy.

"Yeah. I'll be fine. It'll just take a while, is all." I pushed myself away from the demon pole and stood unassisted for a few seconds, to make sure I could. Grinch slapped me on the back to set me on my way and turned back toward his apartment.

The usual ten-minute walk took me close to half an hour, but I made it—dizzy, unsteady, holding on to gates and walls and parked cars. I let myself into my apartment and fell on the mattress. I lay there waiting for the room to stop spinning, before I rolled over and kicked my shoes off. I left my clothes on, dragged myself on my belly toward the pillows, and fell asleep.

The next morning, awakened by the clock-radio alarm at eight-thirty, I found I could not move. Not my arms, not my legs, not my head. Nothing. I was paralyzed. I couldn't reach over and turn off the goddamn radio. I figured the only thing I could do was go back to sleep. I had no other plans for the day. I didn't have to go to work. I let my eyes close and drifted off.

When I awoke an hour later, I hesitated before trying to move my body. What if I couldn't? Would I end up starving to death on this dirty mattress, in this room, my body devoured by wood ants?

Bad thought.

I mustered all the energy I could and wiggled my fingers. They grabbed the edge of the sheet. One by one, I tried wrists, elbows, shoulders. Slow and painful, but I could move them.

I still couldn't move my legs, and my head was spinning. Dizzy as I was, the chances of puking all over myself and the mattress seemed to be running pretty high. It would be best if I got myself to the bathroom.

I shifted my body and reached out for the filthy carpeting. After straining for a minute, my body slid off the mattress to the floor. I was exhausted from the effort. I pulled myself a few feet closer to the bathroom. My head was a nightmare and my legs were useless, but ten minutes later, I felt the cool broken tiles, pushed myself up against the wall near the toilet, and hung my head over the water. What little there was in my belly came rushing out of me.

I reached up, flushed the toilet, and passed out.

When I awoke again and tried to move my head in the least, the nausea rose in my guts, and I retched before passing out again.

This went on all day. Puking and passing out, puking and passing out. In what seemed to be the late afternoon, I heard the front door to the building open and recognized Steve's footsteps tromping upstairs. I couldn't have been happier, curled up on my bathroom floor, to hear him stomping around up there.

I flopped onto the bathroom floor on my belly and crawled out into the other room. I grabbed the cord and pulled the telephone off the desk. I punched Steve's number, heard ringing in the apartment above me, heard stockinged feet slap across the room.

"Hello?"

"Steve? It's Jim," I whispered. "Could you come down here, please?"

"Sure. Why?"

"Long story." I hung up and lay sprawled on the carpet, waiting, trying to remain conscious.

He opened the door and, upon seeing me, understood that my "long story" wasn't very jolly.

"My God! What happened to you?"

"I don't know. I keep passing out and throwing up. I've been in the bathroom the whole day . . . can't move my legs much, I'm dizzy. . . . I got hit in the head pretty bad last night."

Steve phoned for an ambulance, then went outside to wait. A

few long minutes later, two burly men in white stomped into the room, Steve behind them.

"What seems to be the trouble?" one of them asked.

I explained to them what I'd explained to Steve.

"Can you walk?"

"I don't think I can, to be honest."

The two men got on either side of me, and each took an arm.

"Ready . . . one, two . . . *up!*" When they jerked me into the air, my head bobbed to my chest, and the dizziness and nausea swirled back. My legs dangled beneath me, touching the floor out of habit alone.

"Sounds like you've got the flu," one of the men said as they helped me out the door.

"Yeah, flu's goin' around," the other one said.

Flu? What the fuck were they talking about? "Look"— I tried to intervene—"last night I smashed my head on a pole, this morning I can't stand up. . . . What the hell kind of flu is that?"

They dragged me out of the building, in front of which several neighbors and passersby had gathered, curious to see who would be dragged out this time. When they saw who it was, just another guy drunk or stoned, they continued about their business, bored by the spectacle.

My two helpers got me down the steps and over to the ambulance, only then opening the back and sliding out a stretcher.

"Here, lie down," one of them said. They were pissed to have been called away from their canasta game to pick up a damn college kid with the flu. They slammed me into the back of the ambulance and we sped away. I did what I could to keep the bile down while the driver got on the radio.

"This is unit three-seven-two. . . . We are arriving with a male, approximately twenty years of age, exhibiting flulike symptoms. . . ." The fellow on the other end of the radio enjoyed a mighty chuckle over this.

We arrived at the hospital and I was rolled into an examination room and laid out on a table, where I waited and ran inventory again. My head was screaming, but I was able to move my legs. A doctor appeared and gave me a once-over and asked what had happened. I recounted the story again, the pole, the dizziness, the paralysis, the passing out, the puking.

He listened to my heartbeat, pulled the stethoscope out of his ears, and make a note on a chart. "Well," he sighed, bored, "sounds like the flu to me. I think it's safe to let you go home."

I gave up. I had the flu. *Jesus.*

A nurse helped me into a wheelchair, and while I sat upright, I kept my head bowed. Trying to raise it brought the nausea back. The nurse wheeled me to the lobby and stopped.

"I'm going to leave you here until your ride home arrives," she chirped.

Ride? I didn't have a ride. I didn't know anyone with a car. I didn't even know anyone with a *bike.* It looked as if I was going to be sitting there a long time. I closed my eyes and drifted off.

I was awakened sometime later by another nurse. "Hey," she whispered, "you don't look so hot. You sure you're ready to go home?"

I shook my head weakly.

"I know where to take you." She pushed me down several long hallways until she found the door she was looking for. "You'll be fine here." She opened the door into an examination room, helped me out of the chair and onto the bed. "Just rest here for a while."

She shut off the lights before she left, and as I lay there in darkness I assumed she was my angel. The one who finally recognized that there was something terribly wrong with me, and who was going to find a doctor who wouldn't dismiss me as a whiner and a fool. But then I realized that no doctors were coming.

Some two hours later, the lights snapped back on.

"Okay, you!" the same nurse sang out. "Did you get some rest? Good. You can go home now."

I had given up wondering or hoping. She set me into the wheelchair and rolled me back down the hallway, only to leave me right where she had found me, so I could wait for my ride.

I waited a few minutes before trying to stand. I hobbled out the front doors, then slowly hobbled my way home.

A FEW BLOCKS from my apartment was a small clinic, so the next day I called for an appointment. Maybe someone there could find out what was wrong with me. While I had regained use of my limbs, and while the puking and passing out had mostly subsided, I couldn't walk a straight line to save my life.

The doctor at the clinic gave me the usual once-over and asked me the usual questions, and I told my usual story, this time emphasizing the blow to the head.

"Did I tell you about the steel lamppost?"

"Yes, yes, you did."

It was this doctor's conclusion that I had too much wax in my ears. He led me from his office to an examination room, pulled a giant syringe out of a drawer, and flushed out both ears. Granted, there was a helluva lot of wax in there, huge chunks of material washed into his bowl, but I felt no better afterward (though I could hear better). He sent me on my way, as the others before him had, satisfied that he had done his job and done it well.

That afternoon, I consulted the yellow pages for neurologists.

By the end of the afternoon, I had an appointment set with a doctor whose office was in a building on the outskirts of town.

Meanwhile, I still had work to contend with, and my dizziness wasn't abating. My fellow employees at the porn shop took great glee in asking me to retrieve something for them from the far end of the store or on a high shelf. They would watch me stagger off the foot-high platform in front of the cash register and careen across the stained, once red carpeting into tabletops full of half-price dildos and cut-rate packs of used flesh magazines, down narrow aisles packed with proof upon proof that the End Times were near. Oh, how they laughed!

For my first appointment with the neurologist, Steve had agreed to come with me. We took a cab ten miles out to a stark, modern gray medical building. We were the only two in the waiting room. Still, we had to wait more than an hour before the doctor arrived.

A small woman with short, mousy hair and hard features stepped quickly across the room to where we were sitting. She looked from one of us to the other and finally said, "You must be Jim."

"Yeah."

"I could tell by the way you were sitting."

Steve was leaning back in a soft chair, relaxed, flipping through a magazine. I was teetering forward on the edge of my seat, nervous that if I leaned back I might not be able to get up.

"Come with me." She jerked me up by the hand and led me into a hallway lined with doors. There was nobody else around. Suddenly, she stopped.

"Okay, I want to try something here," she said.

"Uh-huh?"

"Stand facing me." I did. She was a few inches shorter than I was, and I looked down at her, without the slightest notion what to expect. She put one hand on each of my shoulders, and in a flash spun me around three times and pushed me down the hall away from her.

I made it three steps, maybe four, before crashing into the wall and collapsing into a heap. I lay like a slaughtered lamb, waiting for her to come over and kick me to see if I was dead. Instead, she approached me, looked down, and said:

"Wow, that was pretty bad."

She took me to an examination room, where she ran the same tests and asked the same questions the other doctors had, and I told the same story. I told her also about the doctors who had seen me over the course of the week and their diagnoses: a nasty case of the flu, a severe ear wax problem.

She listened patiently, nodding and taking notes, then asked me to tell her again about the lamppost. Where had it struck my head, and how had I felt immediately afterward?

Finally, someone believed me?

After a few more questions and a few more tests ("Follow my finger with your eyes"; "Stand on one foot"), she scheduled me for an EEG and an MRI, to ascertain if the blow to my head had caused a concussion or established a permanent imprint on my brain.

A week later, the test results in, the neurologist called with her findings: Nothing. Nothing at all. She had no idea what to make of what had happened to me.

"That dizziness should pass before too long," she told me.

"I figured that," I replied.

"Maybe it's your inner ear. Perhaps you jarred it when you hit the pole."

I thanked her for her time and hung up.

A few weeks later, the dizziness passed, just as she had said it would, and I forgot about it.

NEAR THE END of my shift at the porn shop one Thursday night in late spring, Grinch came through the front door. I could tell by his tight, jerky movements that he was excited about something. Either that or he'd lucked into some crystal meth. He stormed toward me, slapped both palms on the counter, then picked up his right hand and pointed at me.

"You're in a band!" he yelled, and stood back for my response.

"Okay."

"In this morning's mail," he announced proudly, "I received, free of charge, without requesting it, in my very own name, a Sears credit card."

"Christ, Grinch—the *fools*. Don't they . . . ?"

"Yes, sir. You know what I did? I hopped on a bus and rode straight out to the nearest Sears catalogue outlet, and I flipped through that big catalogue of theirs, and you know what I got?"

"Children's clothes."

"Better. I got us a gee-tar, an amplifier, a microphone, a Casio, and a music stand. We're in a band!"

"A music stand? Grinch, do you know how to read music or play any instrument at all?"

"Nosir, and neither do you. We'll be the greatest band the world has ever seen!"

"Or at least the most obnoxious."

Two weeks later, I was working an afternoon shift when Grinch burst through the front door again in a state of high agitation. "Stop by my apartment when you get off here," he said.

I nodded and kept ringing up the sale I was working on. "I'll be there. 'Bout six-thirty."

When I arrived, we started planning. First and foremost, we needed a name.

" 'The Grand Inquisitors,' " Grinch declared.

"Been taken. They're a bad metal band out of Georgia."

"Okay."

"How about 'The Wolf Man, the Rat Man, and the Psychotic Dr. Schreber'?" I suggested. It was the subtitle to Freud's *Three Case Histories.*

"But there are only two of us."

"Forgot."

"Howzabout 'Bad Karma'?"

In contrast to the swiftness with which we named the Nihilist Workers' Party, this process went on for days, until Grinch remembered a line from David Lynch's film version of *Dune.* "Restore spice production," one character orders, "or you will spend the rest of your days in a pain amplifier!" That said it all. We wanted to amplify the pain of innocent bystanders. Better still, we wanted to see if people would pay to have their pain amplified.

Realizing that we didn't have a percussion section, we went to look for supplies in an abandoned railway corridor not too far from Grinch's. We wandered down the tracks and around empty boxcars, looking for anything that might make an interesting noise. Most of the metal scraps were too thick or too flat and made only a tinny thud when you whacked them with another piece of metal. Then we stumbled on a caboose chimney, about ten feet long, tin, the metal at the ends twisted, sharp and dangerous. When struck with the railroad coupling we'd found, it made a gorgeous, crashing sound that carried farther than any normal drum kit ever could. We hoisted it on our shoulders and carried it to Grinch's apartment, and set it up in a corner.

Before our instruments arrived, we arranged our debut inside a club. First week of June, at O'Cayz Corral, the only place in town that would have us. While most bands had to turn in demo tapes and audition for a gig, we got one by the sheer demonic force of Grinch's charisma.

When the Sears instruments arrived, we were ready. I got to Grinch's place after work and found that he had pulled most everything out of the boxes. His floor was a deep mess of wires, cables, cheap electronics, and torn cardboard. He sat in the middle of it all, sticking various plugs into assorted outlets and seeing what would happen.

"I think this will work now," he said as he plugged the cord from the cheap brown guitar into the amplifier. He hit the strings and stared at the amp. Nothing.

I opened a beer. "Grinch, is the amp plugged into anything?"

He gave me a look, pulled the guitar from around his neck, set it on a cardboard box, found the cord on the back of the amp, dragged it across the floor, and plugged it in. A red light on the amp came on, and a snap of feedback echoed away.

He strapped the guitar back on and strummed it again. This time a distorted, crackling buzz issued from the amp. We were in business.

Over the next few hours, we tried plugging everything into the amp. We fiddled with knobs and buttons, generating as ugly a sound as possible.

"The thing about the old Moogs," Grinch said, as I was toying with the dozens of buttons on the Casio, "is that you had to be extremely talented in order to make them sound good. With these things," he gestured to the keyboard, which played the cheesiest of rhythms all by itself quite well, "is that you have to be extremely talented to make them sound *bad.*"

By ten, we were ready to try out a song.

In the previous day's mail I had received a New Age book catalogue. The New Age philosophy behind it, though, was two-fisted, ugly, and perverse. The folks who put it together were less interested in healing crystals, past-life regression, and aromatherapy than they were in UFOs, Bigfoot, and visions of Christ appearing on waffles and barn doors. We culled lyrics to a dozen songs from that catalogue.

I stood at the microphone and flipped randomly through the pages to an ad for a book about monsters. I gave Grinch the sign to start, and we began. While he banged away at the guitar and I hit the buttons on the keyboard for a slow, grinding *thukka-thukka*, I read:

> *Near the Elizabeth, New Jersey, entrance*
> *To the New Jersey Turnpike,*
> *Several youths reported encountering*
> *"The biggest man we ever saw."*
> *He was about seven feet tall, dark-complexioned,*
>   *and had little round eyes*
> *Set far apart.*
> *At first he had his back to the boys,*
> *But as they approached*
> *He pivoted around*
> *Stared right at the boys,*
> *And then he grinned.*

We called that first Pain Amplifiers' song "The Grinning Man."

Over the next three months, the NWP all but vanished, subsumed by the Pain Amplifiers. We played shows around Madison, indoors, where we were expected, and outdoors, where we weren't. We took a Greyhound to Chicago and played a short impromptu set at O'Hare, then went on to Hyde Park, where we'd been invited to play, and attracted an audience of two.

After our third song, the pair of punk rock girls approached the stage. "When are you guys going to play something we could dance to?" one of them asked.

"I think we could arrange that," Grinch told her, smiling his devil smile. "All you had to do was ask."

With our Casio, all we had to do was hit a few keys for it to play a perfect disco song. I punched the necessary buttons, and Grinch and I left to get a drink.

We had big plans. We recorded a four-song demo tape in a friend's attic and sent copies to the big record labels. We didn't hear back from a single one. We hand-delivered a copy of the tape to a radio station; a DJ put it on the air and turned it off a minute into the first song. We left copies on consignment at record stores and sold a total of two, to friends. A friend who was on a radio talk show put in a plug for us. He called our music "ontopraxiological rock 'n' roll with that di-bungy-whompa-whompa beat." We had no idea what he meant, but we were glad to adopt it as our signature description, and used it whenever we could.

Grinch and I ended the few shows we played by throwing the caboose chimney into the audience. This won us enough of a reputation that we were offered the opening slot when our musical heroes, a heavy-metal band called the Mentors, came to town.

The Mentors, three fat L.A. bikers who performed in executioner hoods, had been virtually unknown beyond the tightest of punk rock circles, although they had several records out. But during the Parents Music Resource Center hearings in the mid-eighties, Tipper Gore brought them instant notoriety by citing and reciting their lyrics as perfect examples of the kind of garbage that children needed to be protected from. " 'Bend up and smell my anal vapors,' " she hesitantly read to the members of a Senate subcommittee, " 'your face is my toilet paper.' "

The Mentors even offended us every once in a while. Getting the opening spot for their show was a tremendous honor.

The Mentors' founder, drummer, and song stylist was El Duce, an ugly, obese toad with a remarkable natural sense of poetics. He was an idiot savant when it came to creating rhymes so obvious no one had ever dared rhyme them. After thousands of years of civilization's waiting, it took El Duce to rhyme "woman from Sodom" with "takes it up the bottom."

The day of the show, we got to the club early to set up. An hour before we were supposed to go on, we heard that the Mentors were still in Chicago and had no idea how to get to Madison, let alone the club. That was problem number one.

Problem number two was T.

T was a former Green Beret who had left the military, apparently, in order to become a Nazi skinhead. At two hundred fifty pounds of angry muscle, bone, and tattoo ink, he was notorious around the city for his explosive temper and feats of cruel strength. He had put more than one uppity frat boy in the hospital after they tried to impress their girlfriends by taking him on.

T was also a huge Mentors fan, but he couldn't afford the cover charge. When Tom, the owner of the club, refused to let him in for free or earn his way in by working the front door that night, T got an idea.

"Why don't you guys let me sing one of your songs tonight?" he asked Grinch and me, as we sat at the bar. "That way I could say I'm with you guys, and I'd get in."

Normally it would have been fine, but this was our moment of glory.

"I don't know, T," Grinch said, as gently as possible. "This show is really important to us and all. . . ."

"You're saying I'd ruin it?" T glared down at Grinch.

"No, not that."

"What, then?"

I kept my mouth shut and took another pull on my beer. I wasn't going to get into this, no sir.

"We'll see how the show goes. You tell Tom you're with us, that you helped us carry equipment or something, and we'll see about letting you sing."

"You'd better." T slammed his empty mug onto the bar and strode out the front door.

"What are we in for now?"

"It'll be fine," Grinch assured me.

"We're going to be killed, aren't we?"

"Probably."

We put our minds back on the show. If we got killed in the middle of it by a Nazi skinhead gone berserk, at least we'd make the news.

The club was packed by the time we were supposed to go on. That was something we weren't used to. What's more, it was an angry crowd of punks, bikers, skinheads. Cheerful, happy, well-adjusted people didn't go to see the Mentors; those people stayed home and locked their doors whenever the Mentors were around. As we set up, anger and hatred hung palpably in the stale club air. There was going to be trouble.

When we got onstage, the crowd quieted down. Grinch reached into a bag he was carrying and threw into the audience two fistfuls of packets we'd grabbed the day before from a big fishbowl of free condoms at Planned Parenthood.

"Here, take these home with ya, ya bastards!" he yelled into the microphone. "We don't care whether you get AIDS!"

I leaned over to the mike. "No, we just don't want you to breed."

A shower of condoms and cigarettes and beer flew back at us. We got the equipment going and started banging away. We had worked out a batch of songs by this time, songs like "Superbowl Sunday," "Blood-Sucking Freaks," and "Thuggery and Buggery"—all too long, all intolerable, most of them based on found texts. We'd even worked up one cover song, the Ed Ames classic "My Cup Runneth Over," which we had heard on the easy-listening station.

After forty-five minutes of ugliness, we were down to our last few songs. I was beginning "Nowhere, Nothin' Fuckup" when something yanked my legs out from under me and slammed me to the stage, hard. A moment later, there was a mountain on top of me.

It was T. Our set was almost finished, and we hadn't invited him up to sing. I wasn't thinking about that at the time. All I knew was that something was planted on my back and had a hold of my hair and was using it to slam my head against the stage, repeatedly.

I was pinned by an enormous weight backed by Special Forces training. The only thing that saved me was the fact that Grinch had his blessed railroad coupling in his hands. He started beating on T's head as T beat on mine. The crowd screamed for blood. Anybody's. The Casio merrily doodled along as my skull kept hitting the filthy wooden stage.

Grinch knocked T back, finally, and he relented. I rolled over to see him standing above me, raising his arms in victory to the delirious crowd. I stood up, shaky, battered, bloodied, but surprisingly not in such bad shape after being assaulted by Sasquatch.

We ended the show as our adventure had begun, with an extended version of "The Grinning Man," which drove the audience out onto the sidewalk. Then we stopped. We broke down the equipment and moved it to the back of the club while everyone waited for El Duce and his crew to show up.

The Mentors eventually made it, hungover, exhausted, and junk-sick. The more Duce insulted the crowd, the more they loved him. He was too damn cute in his grotesquerie to take it seriously. Deep in his heart, deep in that expansive gut of his, he was a sweetie-pie. Even as he called us "New Wave faggots" and "sissy-boy posers."

When it was over, at three in the morning, I sat at a table inside the club, waiting for Grinch to show up with a truck so we could get all our shit home without having to carry it again.

"Hey, Slack." The club owner tapped me on the shoulder. "You gotta get your gear out on the sidewalk, I'm locking up."

"No problem." I touched the swelling wounds around my eyes and forehead. Then I got up and dragged the chimney to the front door.

"You know," the owner said, as I was returning for another load, "people came out here tonight to see a mean, nasty, disgusting show—and you guys gave it to them."

"Why, thank you, Tom," I told him. "That's very nice of you." We shook hands.

I was still waiting for Grinch when El Duce came out of the club.

"Proud to have opened for you, Duce," I said.

He stopped his weary shuffle and turned to me, baggy Hawaiian shorts hanging too low, enormous beer belly drooping to the sidewalk. He stuck out a callused hand and grabbed mine.

"You're a real American, Slackjaw," he barked. "Keep on a-*rockin'*!"

"I will, Duce." He was the best. When Duce said something like, "Keep on a-rockin'," you knew he meant it.

But what I answered him that night would prove untrue. I didn't keep on a-rockin'. That was the last Pain Amplifiers show. It was time to move on.

d a n   r a t h e r

I HAD BEEN carrying things—books, clothes, the sundry what-not of a small life—from the truck into my new place for about an hour when the door of the apartment next to mine flew open.

Standing in the doorway was something that must have been human at one time. Its mouth hung open, revealing two jagged teeth dangling in a dark maw, globs of dried white spittle at the corners. The skin on its face was pulled tight, cracked and dry; the eyes were sunken and black. What hair there was drooped in wispy tangled knots. It wore a torn bathrobe that might have long ago been pink. Its feet were bare. With its left hand, it thrust an envelope at me.

"Can you put this in the mailbox for me?" it croaked.

"Sure." Sore and tired, I wiped the sweat from my brow and took the envelope, eager to finish moving. I hated moving.

"My name's Ruth," the creature croaked again, "and I'm *a hundred and thirty-five years old*." The voice was wracked and hoarse and ragged. Dry as the skin on her face. Her voice alone made me believe she was telling the truth.

"Well, I'll be," I said, not knowing what else to say to an introduction like that. "My name's Jim, and uh, I'm moving in next door." I gestured at the open doorway a few feet down the hall. I didn't want it to seem like an invitation.

"Can you put that in the mailbox for me?" she asked again, jabbing a skinny bent finger at the envelope I had already taken from her.

"Sure," I repeated, and nodded absently. I looked at the envelope and turned it over. "Wait a minute," I told my new friend. "I can't mail this for you. You didn't put a stamp on it yet."

Ruth stared at me.

"It don't need a stamp," she said, firm and proud. "It's going to Dan Rather."

I focused on the address. Scrawled in pencil across the front of the yellowed envelope was:

> Dan Rather
> CBS News
> New York

No zip code, no street address. Ruth seemed to have interpreted Mr. Rather's nightly signoff as an announcement of his mailing address for fans and well-wishers.

I stood staring at the address, befuddled and exhausted, when her door slammed shut and the lock snapped into place. I put the envelope in my back pocket and went about my business.

Later that afternoon, rental truck empty, new apartment littered with boxes, I rummaged through several cartons until I found a virgin bottle of scotch and a box of Phillies Titans. I cracked the bottle open, poured a shot into a plastic cup, lit up a fat cigar, and popped a Residents cassette into my crummy tape player. *Walter Westinghouse went to town and found a friend today.* . . . I stepped around some boxes and looked out my window. Another alley, another blank brick wall staring back at me from fifteen feet away. It was the same with every apartment I'd lived in. I raised a toast to it all.

I had accepted an invitation from the University of Minnesota to attend graduate school in Minneapolis. What else could a young man with a philosophy degree do but go to grad school?

The university's Humanities Department was launching a new program, Comparative Studies in Discourse and Society, and I was one of six students in the inaugural year. The faculty consisted of people from English, German, philosophy, history, women's studies, comparative literature, everywhere. The program sounded like a confusing jumble of inchoate ideas, but then again, so was I, and it seemed like a match.

I had moved from an awful apartment in Madison to an apartment smack in the heart of what Minneapolites would call a slum. I had seen worse, I had lived in worse, but this was about as bad as Minneapolis got.

Over the next few weeks, as I became situated, I found myself glancing at the floor outside Ruth's apartment whenever I locked my door on the way out. Four or five days a week there would be a stampless envelope in the hallway outside her door. Always addressed to Dan Rather, at the same hopeless address. And always I'd pick it up as I passed by and stick it in a mailbox for her.

One day when I was feeling grumpy and curious, I didn't dutifully mail it for her. Instead I carried the envelope around with me all day, brought it back to my apartment that night, and opened it. What could a one-hundred-thirty-five-year-old woman have to say to Dan Rather day after day, week after week?

Inside the envelope were four sheets of crisp yellowed paper, covered front and back with the same shaky pencil scrawl as on the envelope. The paper smelled vaguely of shit. My reward for the small evil act of stealing an old woman's mail was a detailed account of Ruth's first lesbian encounter, in an outhouse, when she was seven years old, which ended when her father walked in on the scene.

I filed the letter away and looked forward to the next one. Most of her letters weren't that good. "Saw a mouse today," she would write. "He came to the middle of the room and nibbled on some crumbs. Then he went away." Every so often she folded a little cash in with her letter. That was always a nice surprise. Given what I was living on, I was happy to accept it.

The more I read her letters, the more I was able to piece her story together. Ruth's son had put her up in the apartment some time back; now he stopped by only once a month, with groceries. Ruth was expected to take care of the rent herself with her Social Security, unless she wanted to go to a home. The television, and thus Mr. Rather, were all she had.

Ruth continued her correspondence, and I dove into my work as a grad student. Each quarter I was required to instruct an "Introduction to Humanities" course. I had ten weeks to teach a hundred fifty students everything that happened in literature, music, science, and art between 1700 and the present. I tried hard to keep my lectures interesting and funny, but nothing will crush your enthusiasm quicker than attempting to explain Voltaire, Marx, and *Heart of Darkness* to an auditorium full of dead eyes. There were occasional sparks of hope, a handful in each class, but by and large it was hopeless.

What disturbed me most about teaching was standing in front of these students, giving them information, then asking them to write a paper about what I had told them, only to have my own words regurgitated back to me. Not only regurgitated, but re-gurgitated slightly skewed:

"Marx felt that history was in the past."

"Nietzsche's sister married an anti-semantic" (or alterna-tively, an "anti-semiotic").

"In *Heart of Darkness*, Conrad is relating to the readers Marlowes discovery of the dangers that freedom and powder can have on people."

"The nineteenth century was characterized by a resurgence of new ideas."

" 'In Memorium' is a poem that could easily be put into a up beat song and, unless you were concentrating on the words, you could experience a very happy feeling."

"The poem argued for carpe diem—that is, 'cease the day.' "

I called this font of information my "Whiz-Dumb."

BEFORE GRAD SCHOOL, before I had even left the University of Chicago in 1984 to move to Madison, I'd started talking to a woman named Laura. That in itself was something, as neither of us ever talked to much of anyone. Laura was brilliant and enigmatic, with long brown hair and a beautiful, soft face. Except for her eyes: they were hard, among the hardest I'd seen.

Though she carried herself with a certain anger and bitterness, I was able to make her laugh the first time we spoke. And once I heard her throaty laughter, I was hooked. After I moved to Madison, I besieged her with letters, and she wrote back a few times. That was good enough for me. I'd call her now and then, but for the most part, ours was just a friendly correspondence.

When I felt settled in Minneapolis, I invited her for a weekend, to get her out of Chicago for a few days. She had had a rough go of it, and I thought she could use a vacation. I'd bought two tickets for a Tom Waits show in a cheap attempt at persuasion. To my surprise, it worked.

"I didn't really think you would come," I told her when she showed up at my door on a Friday night.

"Neither did I," she replied, "but the folks at the office thought it would be good for me."

"Swell."

We ordered a pizza and I opened a bottle of scotch.

I had high hopes for that weekend, but things turned strange

pretty damn quick. It was close to Halloween, and in preparation for the trick-or-treaters, I'd put together a basket of goodies to hand out. Little bundles of cigarettes tied with festive black and orange ribbons.

Laura didn't think that was funny at all.

"Oh, it is a *little* bit funny," I argued.

"No it's not."

We fell into a weekend-long debate about personal morality and basic ethics. We walked around the city; I took her to art museums and a park. At the park, we started feeding popcorn to the ducks, arguing all the while, and ended up hurling the popcorn at each other instead. I remember long, tension-filled silences and depressive fits.

It was love all right, though neither of us dared admit it.

She didn't tell me until the last minute Sunday night that her flight would be leaving before the concert. As she got into the cab for the airport, we looked at each other. The walls slid away, the anger evaporated, and we reached for each other.

Two weeks after Laura left, the demons returned to my head, this time unexpectedly. I had not noticed the pressure building. I woke up one morning, put my coat on, stepped outside, and strolled around downtown Minneapolis, stopping in each drugstore I passed, stealing as many boxes of over-the-counter sleeping pills as would fit into my coat pockets. Once my pockets were filled, I stopped by my apartment to empty them, then headed out for more pills.

WHEN I CAME TO, I was sitting in bed, straining against the straps that held me down, shouting in German to no one in particular.

I'm in a hospital. I'm in a hospital and I'm strapped down and

*I'm screaming in German. Why, I must be insane! I won't have
to do anything more for the rest of my life! All I have to do is keep
saying silly things and I'll be fed, I'll be taken care of, I'll be able
to read and write! This is great!*

Then my education caught up with me.

If I can think that, then I must not be insane.

Damn.

I opened my eyes and found myself in the intensive care ward
of the Hennepin County Medical Facility, with my parents sitting at the foot of the bed, where they had been waiting and hoping for three days that I would come out of my delirium.

My mother was crying quietly, and my dad, who was scared
of nothing in this world, looked terrified.

"Hi, you two," I said.

All sorts of tubes were stuck into my body. There were two in
each arm, a catheter screwed into my penis, and tubes leading
Lord knows where under the sheets. After learning that the overdose of sleeping pills and scotch had made my kidneys shut down,
after a day of talking to my parents and attempting to compre-
hend the cubicle I was strapped into, I realized that my contact
lenses were still in. It must've been close to a week by this time.
If they stayed in too long, they would dissolve on the misshapen
globes of my eyeballs.

I asked for a lens case and some solution, which were brought
to me by a brusque, fuzzy nurse.

Peeling the plastic from my eyes, I saw a clump of white at
the foot of my bed.

"Jim?"

"Yeah."

"Hi, Jim. My name is Dr. Tomlinson. I've been taking care of
you since you've been in here."

"Good for you, Doc."

"We thought we'd lost you there for a while."

"You did. That was the whole idea."

"Yes, well, I have a group of students here with me, and we were wondering if we could ask you a few questions."

I didn't have anything else to do. After the typical "Count backward" and "Who's the president?" requests, someone finally asked: "Why'd you do it?"

I fidgeted around on the bed, but the wires and tubes and needles and straps held me firmly.

"Good question," I said, aiming my eyes in the general direction of the voice. "And utterly unanswerable. I could lie to you, say something banal like, 'My parents locked me in a dishwasher until I was sixteen,' but I'm a terrible liar."

"Good, so try to tell us the truth the best you can." Tomlinson's voice again.

I thought about it.

"Call it a genetic imperative. Call it *boredom.* Every year or so, every eighteen months, things build up. I don't understand what or why, but they do. And I try to off myself. It's a catharsis. I always feel much better afterward. Problem is, every time I try, I get closer to the real thing. This time I guess I got pretty fucking close."

"What sorts of things are you talking about, the things that build up?"

"Christ, I don't know. Buying groceries. Paying phone bills. Sweeping the floor. Buying deodorant. Walking home from the bus. Just living is such a pain in the ass, sometimes, you know? All these things people do without thinking about it? Sometimes I can't *stop* thinking about it. There it is, right in front of me. There's no escaping it. I'm doing things I have to do, there's no escaping doing them, and there I am, doing them. Just rather not have to anymore, I guess." I paused to think about what I'd just said. "In a way, it's not insanity at all. I'm perfectly sane. It scares me. And suicide seems a perfectly sane response to a banal world." I don't know if they got what I was saying or not, or if they figured these were the ramblings of a crazy man. The med students and I chatted, exchanged pleasant nothings, for another half-hour.

Ten days later, after the tubes were unceremoniously yanked out of me, a nurse helped me into a wheelchair and pushed me to the hospital's locked-door psych ward, where I spent the next several weeks.

When I was released from the madhouse this time, my parents, who had stayed in Minneapolis and visited me every other day, drove me back to my apartment.

I got out of the car, thanked them for the ride, and went inside, abandoning them there at the curb. Once inside, I started thinking. Thinking more than I had in a long time.

When I had left for Chicago, I left my folks behind, hardly talking to them at all, unless I wanted to borrow money, which I didn't do often. When I went home for a weekend every couple of months, although it was clear they were thrilled to have their son home again, I hardly spoke to them; I spent most of my time running around Green Bay. I was so wrapped up in the external craziness and the internal madness I'd found in Chicago and Madison, this new life I was forging, that I had unconsciously severed the ties to my old life. I had forgotten about it. I had forgotten about them. But they hadn't forgotten me.

These people had driven five hours in the middle of the night after the hospital called, just to sit by my bedside. They never left that bedside for three days. And now I was about to blow them off again? Time and again as I was growing up, my dad told me, "Everything else will fall away. Your friends will leave, your situations will change. But your family will always be here." He'd proved himself right over these past several weeks.

They were staying with my dad's sister Dorthea, just outside of town. I looked up her number and called, asking her to tell them, once they got there, to turn around and come back to my place. I didn't tell her anything else.

An hour and a half later, there was a knock at the door. From their frightened expressions I could tell they thought I was losing my mind again.

I let them in. We sat down on the couch, and I told them I was sorry. I had been a bad kid. For years I had been a bad kid, and I had hurt them. I knew that now. I didn't want to do that anymore; I loved them too much.

What I told them was true, and from that moment on, we stayed in close contact. We became good friends again. My apology, however, didn't extend to the rest of the world.

I WAS WELCOMED BACK into the graduate program to continue my studies a few days later. Nobody said a word about what had happened. The only thing that had changed, really, was my attitude, which had left the locked-door ward hardened and cruel. I was tired of writing papers about papers other people had written about books other people had written about some cultural icon or work of art. I was having serious doubts about a future in academia. It was a world that was just too damn small.

My concerns about school were affecting my judgment outside school, where I needed to be sharp. I was still shaky from the institution; my body had not fully recovered from the overdose, and my mind tended to wander in the middle of things. I had to get back into practice with my extracurricular activities. What had been petty shoplifting just for kicks in Madison exploded into a way of life once I moved north.

If you take up thievery, or con artistry, or confidence games

of any kind, you realize that Americans are among the most
blindly trustful people in the world. They may install security
alarms, video surveillance systems, double locks, and scanners in
their homes and stores, but once they install them, they forget
them. People give themselves over to the technology, believing
circuitry will guard and protect them.

There was a bookstore in St. Paul, a nice place, tucked in the
basement of a dead plastic downtown shopping complex. I had
poked around there a few times and seen things that I wanted
very much but couldn't imagine affording. I did buy a book there
once, to see if the sales clerk would deactivate a magnetic strip
in it before giving it back to me. But it wasn't clear.

I waited a few days after this reconnaissance visit, wrote a
quick script for myself, and gave the store a call. Someone answered halfway through the first ring.

"Good morning, Odeon Books."

"Hello, I was wondering if I might be able to speak to a man-
ager, please."

"That would be me."

"Oh, great. What's your name, sir?"

"Warner. Don Warner."

"Mr. Warner, my name is Andrew Belis and I represent Pattern
Security Systems. We equip stores with electronic antitheft devices. Tell me, is your store set up with any such equipment right
now? Videocameras, alarms, scanners, that type of thing?"

"No, no we're not. Right now I just train my employees to
keep a careful eye out for shoplifters."

"Well, as you might know, bookstores are a primary target for
shoplifters. Millions of dollars' worth of merchandise is stolen
every year from bookstores across the country. A lot of bookstores
right here in St. Paul, maybe even yours, are included. But with
a Pattern system, we can reduce your losses to virtually nothing.

Would you be interested in having me stop by to give you a free estimate as to how much it would cost to equip your store with top-of-the-line antitheft devices?"

"No, thanks. I think I'm doing all right as is. But if you'd like to send me some brochures, I'd be happy to take a look at them, maybe for later."

"Great. Mr. Warner, I think you'll see that a Pattern system is the best thing you could do for yourself. Now let me make sure I have your address correct. . . ."

When we'd finished our business, I threw on my coat and hat and went to the bookstore. On my way in I nodded to Mr. Warner, who was talking to one of his employees behind the counter (probably about keeping an eye out for shoplifters). I moved from the literature section to the philosophy section to the architecture section, then out the door again. There were no bells or whistles.

Once outside, I opened my coat, emptied my pockets, and rearranged the six books I had grabbed. My reading for the next month.

Minneapolis–St. Paul was, is, a clean, white, big midwestern town. When I was living there, all the things the beautiful blond folks didn't like congregated on a single block, Block H of Hennepin Avenue, which stretched between 8th and 9th streets. That's where the bums, dealers, junkies, whores, porn shops, and killer bars were to be found. I spent most of my free time there. With everything bad crushed into that block, the rest of the city was open, soft prey. I simply took what I needed.

I DECIDED TO LEAVE academics for good after attending my first Comparative Studies in Discourse and Society conference. Conferences elevate the reputation of a program and let people know what it's all about. To make a splash in the world of post-toastie criticism, CSDS sponsored one entitled "The Economy of Celebrity," and people came from across the country for it. Since this was a chance for the Humanities Department to show off how bright its grad students were, we were of course invited to a party for conference attendees at a professor's house the night the conference began. Performing at cocktail parties is central to the grad school experience.

One of the other grad students, Lefty, offered to give me a ride. Lefty and I got along. He was funny and smart and a petty thief himself on top of it. When we showed up, already half drunk, the house was crowded, with smart people talking about smart things, using cheekfuls of jargon that was still beyond me. After an hour of making the rounds, the two of us were cornered by the stars of the conference, a husband-and-wife team. We asked them what their presentations were going to be about, and they told us. They asked us what our specialties were, and we told them. There was a long, embarrassing silence. We had nothing more to say to each other.

The next week I went to see Richard, the reigning department chair.

"I'm glad you came in today," he said before I had a chance to tell him what was on my mind. "We have—meaning the rest of the faculty and I—been talking about you."

"Uh-huh."

"For the most part, everyone's happy with your work here. John loved your *Eraserhead* paper, and everything you have given me has been real top-notch."

"Yeeaaahhh . . .?" I didn't have to say "But what?" after that. He'd take care of that for me.

"But we're thinking that your . . . life-style . . . is simply not one befitting an academic."

I didn't bother asking what he meant. I wasn't going to make him explain. I knew. And he knew that I knew. He had saved me the trouble of telling him I was leaving, of saying, essentially, "Thanks for all the help and support over the past two semesters, Richard. Fuck you."

That final, conscious decision to leave academics got me to take the life of the cheap criminal—which had begun so quietly in Madison—more seriously. Petty crime had become my new career plan. I was twenty-one, just a kid, but in my addled mind, I was a tough-guy, a bad-ass beyond measure. Grinch would have been proud of me. I had been hanging out with dealers, other thieves, hookers, pimps, a few men who claimed to be murderers. We congregated in the nastiest bar in town, a place called Moby Dick's, on Block H, the only place in town where such a bar could exist. The police raided it and shut it down once a month; it was always open again a few days later.

When I started sporting the brass knuckles I had ordered from an ad in the back of *Soldier of Fortune,* they gave me that extra bit of class the dealers and pimps seemed to respect. Carrying the knuckles was a manly thing, a sign that I didn't need to rely on guns to take care of my business. The truth is that if I had gotten my hands on a gun, I would've stuck it in my mouth and been done with it.

I taped the knuckles to fit my hand. I wasn't afraid of nothing, not with a pound and a half of brass resting comfortably at the bottom of my coat pocket.

A few times a week, depending on the weather and how much course work I had to do, I would step out for a nighttime walk. Maybe swing by Moby's, maybe not. My eyes still had some flash and dance to them, so going to such a place didn't mean certain death (or at least a great deal of pain) the way it would later.

One of these nights—it was late May, the sky was cloudy,

there was no wind, but it was cool enough for me to need my grimy trench coat—I headed out. The setting was perfect for a kid like me, still imagining himself Bogart or Sterling Hayden, ready and anxious for trouble. I walked down 19th to Nicollett as usual, then took Nicollett across the highway into downtown. By this time of night, most of downtown Minneapolis was deserted. Buildings were dark and shops were closed, but the streets were well lit and the sidewalks wide enough for me to avoid unnecessary trouble.

I strolled to 7th Street and crossed to my left, aiming for Hennepin a few blocks over. I slipped a cheap cigar out of my breast pocket, peeled the plastic away, and fired it up. I was a walking cliché. A quick spin around Block H didn't reveal any familiar faces, so I decided to head home.

Instead of going straight to Nicollett again, I followed Hennepin for a few blocks, past the crumbling majesty of the Orpheum theater and the "Used Erotica" shop across the street. I hopped a bus for no good reason and rode around for a while. Lord knows how long. I got off in an area I didn't recognize and wasn't sure about, and started walking. When I turned on a narrow, dark side street, I heard voices. Downtown had been nearly silent, few cars, fewer people. The voices breaking that silence were a surprise.

All I could tell at first was that a man and a woman were having a tussle. I tried to determine where the voices were coming from, maybe the parking garage ahead. The more I listened, the wilder the voices grew. I kept going until I reached an alley. That's where the people were.

"Leave me the fuck alone!"

"C'mon, baby, I got the money—"

"Get away from me!"

If she wasn't a hooker, she certainly dressed like one: the

boots, the purse, the short shorts. In fact, she looked more like a hooker than most Minneapolis hookers did. I couldn't help thinking that it was much too chilly outside to be dressed that way.

He was unmistakable. Balding and fat, loosened tie, ugly ill-fitting suit with a plastic badge dangling from his left lapel. Another conventioneer. The town was always swarming with them. And like so many others, this one was out to have himself a good time, without knowing how or why. I could see that this guy couldn't hold his liquor.

I made the mistake of believing too much in my talents as a bad-ass and stepped into the alley.

"Let her alone."

He had hold of one of her arms and was blocking her escape with his mighty belly. He half turned his head toward me.

"Mind your own fucking business. We're just playing."

"Ma'am?" I asked.

"Get him the hell away from me."

I was in it now.

"Okay, sir, c'mon." I took another few steps toward them. I was trying to remain calm, but my knees and hands were shaking. "Let her go."

"Fuck outta here," he slurred.

I took a few more steps, close enough to reach out my left hand and clap him on the shoulder. "C'mon, sir."

He let go of the woman's wrist and took a clumsy swing at me. I ducked, and he knocked my hat off. Not knowing what else to do, now that the woman had run away, I tossed what was left of my cigar into his face. He swung stupidly again, and missed again.

My fingers easily slid into the knuckles in my right pocket. I pulled my hand out and landed the brass deep in his soft gut.

"Shit." He heaved as he crumpled first to his knees, then to

his side, then over onto his back. It seemed to take a very long time.

I should have stopped there. Unfortunately, my upper brain hadn't regained control yet. I took a step back and landed a shoe in his ribs. He groaned.

Something in my throat was on fire. My mouth tasted of blood and rust. I stepped around him, dropped to my knees in front of his upturned right leg, and pulled my brass-heavy fist back.

His leg snapped like a gunshot when the knuckles hit, about a foot south of the kneecap. I will never forget that sound. He let out a howl like a skewered monkey, and I ran. I ran blindly, trying to find my way home, thinking, *Christ, oh Christ.* When I got to my apartment, I headed for the bathroom and puked hard. Then I poured myself a shot and went to bed. I'd been in scuffles before, but I'd never come out on top. For the first time, I was frightened by what I had become.

The next several days I scoured the papers, afraid that I might have killed him by accident, instead of just breaking his leg. Nothing. I lay low for a week to play it safe.

Even though I had announced a few weeks earlier that I was leaving the graduate program, I still had obligations to fulfill at the university. Course work to finish up and classes to teach. That was the way I did things. When I finally finished those, I was going to move someplace far away. This time, at least, I wouldn't be moving alone.

After I had gotten out of the hospital the previous autumn, the phone calls to and from Laura had become more frequent. I had made a few trips to Chicago to see her. Despite that disastrous weekend in October, things were going well between us.

During one of my visits, we went shopping for her father's birthday. We were in a big downtown department store, wandering between floors for the right gift. When Laura settled on something, I—out of habit—offered to lift it for her, save her the money. She gave me a look that was both cold and shocked.

"I'm not sending my father any stolen merchandise," she whispered.

When we got back to her apartment, Laura sat me down on the floor.

"James," she said, "I love you. But I hate what you do."

It was the first time Laura had told me she loved me. It was also the first hint I had that my life-style might be in danger should we follow through on our plans.

Since we both seemed to be at a crossroads, with me at the end of my academic career and Laura heading off to grad school, moving in together made too much sense. Rent was cheaper that way.

"Okay," I told her after a while. "I'll stop with the stealing once we get wherever we're going." We weren't sure where that would be yet.

NOT LONG AFTERWARD, an eviction notice appeared on my neighbor Ruth's door, which she would never see, as she never went outside. The notice had been up ten days when I heard pounding on her door in the middle of a Saturday afternoon. The pounding grew louder, and I went to my own door and listened. There were at least three voices in the hallway. When a mechanical *crrrack* echoed down the hall, I finally opened my door to see what was going on.

In the hall were Ruth's son, his wife, the building super, the real estate agent who'd rented me my place, and a locksmith, who was just now cutting Ruth's door open. As the bunch of them shoved their way into her apartment, the real estate agent looked at me and said, "Yup, the old lady's going away."

A moment later, four of them carried her out, the locksmith trailing behind. I returned to my apartment and craned my neck out the window. They carried Ruth out the front door and down the steps and into a waiting van, which drove away the moment the back doors were slammed shut.

I don't think Dan Rather sent that van, I thought, as I watched her being driven away to die.

welcome, neighbor

"I'M GETTING BAD PAINS IN MY CHEST. I can't breathe," Laura said.

"It's just a few more hours now," I reassured her. "You've got to try and hold on. We'll stop next chance and get some more coffee, how's that?"

It was five in the morning and Laura had been driving for eighteen hours solid from Minneapolis to Chicago and now east toward Philadelphia in a ramshackle twenty-foot rental truck whose air-conditioning was on the fritz, whose radio wouldn't provide even static, and whose side mirrors flopped in the wind. We were moving to a city neither of us had spent more than a day or two in, into an apartment neither of us had seen.

We had decided a month before that wherever she ended up going to grad school, we would go together. I had no other plans. I would figure out what I was going to do once I got wherever she was going. I was jumping from one void into another.

When Laura found out that she would be going to Penn, I went to Philadelphia to find us an apartment. I was moments away from leaving a deposit on a place in West Philly when my potential new landlord piped up.

"I hope you guys have cats."

"Not yet," I told him. "But we probably will."

"Good. That'll help with the rats."

I put my checkbook back in my pocket, bought a copy of *The Philadelphia Inquirer*, and returned to Minneapolis. We were supposed to be moving in ten days. After a series of pleading phone calls and overnight letters, I signed a lease and mailed it and a check to the landlord two days before we were supposed to move, hoping it wasn't all a cruel hoax.

We were out on the road, Laura driving the whole way because of my night blindness and increasing lack of depth perception and peripheral vision. Only now was I wondering what I had gotten myself into. I had never lived with anyone. Not really, not in this way.

To add to my worries, Laura was angry with me for not helping with the driving. Though I had tried to explain my condition to her, I wasn't sure if she fully understood the implications. My taking the wheel—even for a few minutes—meant certain doom. I stayed on my side of the truck, staring out the window, worried, keeping my eyes open for the next truck stop, where we could get more coffee.

After we arrived in Philadelphia and unloaded the truck, Laura flew back to Chicago. She had to work for another month, until the first of August. She was leaving me to explore this hostile, alien city and, with any luck, find gainful employment.

We were living downtown, so I could walk most anywhere that mattered. Not much mattered. Philly was in desperate times. It was a city where, as I discovered watching the local news, people were slaughtered on the street while the sun was shining. The second day I was there, three eight-year-olds were shot on the street corner outside the place I had almost rented in West Philly. The third day I was there, a garbage truck split in half on the street outside our new apartment, and nobody came to clean up the mountain of rotting filth for a week. The city was like an overgrown Hennepin Block H, but not as much fun.

What's more, all the windows in our apartment, no matter which direction they faced, stared out at brick walls.

I was home at last.

Finding work in Philadelphia was not as easy as finding bums passed out on my stoop. I picked up two weeklies, *City Paper* and the *Welcomat,* in an attempt to find employment. I had started reading alternative weeklies in Chicago; they were a better source for job listings than the dailies. Before I reached the help-wanteds in the back of the Philly papers, though, I read the articles and features, and a thought occurred to me:

I can do better than this.

I had written the occasional manifesto for the NWP, and I had churned out papers for school, but this kind of hack journalism? No, sir. It was never in my plans to be a writer. Of course, when I stop and take a look at the things that *were* in my plans . . .

I pored over the job listings, looking for something I'd be able to tolerate for more than a week. When nothing surfaced, I tossed the papers aside, went into the kitchen, and cracked open a beer. Then I thought about things for a while.

Two hours later, I finished typing a four-page story. It was a record review, with stories mixed in about some of the colorful schizophrenics I had met over the past years. I mailed a copy to both papers, telling myself I'd wait a week, a week and a half, before calling to see what they thought.

Still, rent was due soon and I had no source of income, no savings to fall back on, nothing. I needed something to happen, and soon. One sticky summer afternoon, I answered an ad looking for help at a used-book store in the Reading Terminal Market.

This was a filthy concrete-floored farmer's market, inside what had been the largest single-span train shed ever built. An overpowering stench of rotting vegetables, old grease, and urine hung in the air. It was a concentrated form of the cologne that permeated the city year-round. Since then, both have been cleaned up considerably.

Denny's "bookstore" was a few yards inside the market: three tables, a couple of bookcases, and a raised counter, where he sold magazines and newspapers. To the left of his place was a stand that sold local wines; across the way was a cookie-and-muffin shop. Denny was a tan, wiry bearded man; he wore a baseball cap and a red T-shirt, when I met him, and he was sweating. *At least there's no dress code,* I thought when I saw him.

We shook hands, and he started firing questions at me, as customers browsed around us. I stood uncomfortably, damp from the fifteen-block walk over. They were typical questions at first—experience, references—but before long they took a turn.

"What are your politics?" he asked in a giggly nasal whine.

"Pardon?"

"Your politics. I'm very politically active—I'm a revolutionary—and I just don't think I could hire anyone who's too right-wing."

What could I say? I dredged up a bunch of old Madison stories that seemed to do the trick. When the questions eventually turned to books, I was on safe ground. We shook hands again and I headed home, but I was worried. How much did I really need this job? Maybe I could hang out for another few weeks, find something that was less, I don't know, *stinky.*

When he called that evening and offered me the job, I accepted. You take what you can get. I started the next day.

ON MY FIRST DAY OFF, I contacted the weeklies to see how they liked my story. I called *City Paper* first. It was the slicker operation: four-color covers, the works. I spoke with one of the editors, most of whom, I noticed, had ridiculous names, like Hoke, Edwina, Winnie.

"Hi, this is Jim Knipfel, and about a week ago I . . ."

"I know very well who you are."

"You do? Thanks . . . I guess."

"Why would you *ever* think we'd be interested in this story?"

All I did was mention my name, and suddenly this woman was quivering with rage. It was not exactly the response I had hoped for. Then again, I was new to this business.

"Gee, I guess I thought it was, um, funny?"

"No, it's *not*. I'm sorry, but our readers would not appreciate the attitude you take toward schizophrenics."

"Oh . . . but . . . I say right there, first paragraph, that I prefer the company of schizophrenics to that of normal people. . . ."

"Mr. Nipfel—"

"*Kh*, Knipfel. You pronounce the *k*."

"Well, Mr. *Kah*-nipfel, I happen to have a long line of schizophrenics in my family, and I thought it was cruel."

I had nothing left to lose.

"Well, thanks for reading it anyway. Oh, and tell me, did one of those nut jobs *name* you?"

I hung up and lit a smoke and conjured a few good insults before calling the other paper. When the editor there told me what an awful person I was, I'd tear him a new one.

I flipped through the *Welcomat* again before calling. It was shoddy with a homemade cut-and-paste look. I wondered if it was even worth it.

I called anyway. At least I'd get to yell at someone.

Again, I was put through to the editor.

"Hiya, Mr. Davis?"

"Yeah."

"Hi, Jim Knipfel here . . ."

"Oh, good. I'm glad you called. You didn't put your phone number on the story."

"Why, did you want to call to yell at me?"

"No, why?"

"It's been that kind of a day."

"No. I'm not going to yell at you. I liked your story."

That afternoon I walked to the newspaper's offices, which were hidden in a narrow, crumbling, three-story building in the middle of a narrow, crumbling alleyway that at one time might have been considered a street.

Davis's voice had sounded young on the phone. From the business he was in, I was expecting a hipster with slicked-back hair and a small ponytail, sport jacket over a T-shirt, Italian shoes with no socks. I was prepared for the worst. It was another blistering hot day and I was sweating badly under my hat as I entered the building and went upstairs.

When I turned the corner at the top of the steps, I found Derek Davis sitting behind his desk, beneath a cracked and stained skylight. No ponytail. No sport jacket. No Italian shoes. No shoes at all, as a matter of fact. Just socks.

He stood up and shuffled over to me. A tiny man with a long white beard, a beak of a nose between sharp eyes, and a paunch. He looked like a wizened old troll. We shook hands and set to talking about cities, music, and my story. A week later he ran my first piece. Things were starting to fall into place. It seemed I was beginning to locate a foothold in this new void of mine. Better news still was that Laura would be moving in soon. At least I hoped that was good news. But with two sort-of jobs I could cover my half of the rent.

M Y D A Y J O B at Denny's bookshop provided me contact with a select group of people. Reading Terminal Market was perched on the ragged edge of one of the nastier parts of town, so many of the folks who stumbled through were junkies, criminals, and crackheads. The rent-a-cops who patrolled the floor were there primarily to break up fights and interrupt drug deals. One end of the terminal was controlled by the Amish mob, and another large area by the Italian mob. The corner I was in was controlled by misfits and cast-offs who paid ridiculous rents for the privilege of being there.

The fellow who ran the wine shop was as sweet as he was dim-witted. He was always breaking corks and asking me to get them out of the bottles for him. Before long, we made a deal: If I got a cork out of a bottle, he would give me two bottles in payment. I went a good eight months without having to buy a bottle. When their boss was gone, the cookie people across the way would give me a sackful, just because they liked me better than Denny. Denny scared the bejeezus out of them. So I always had a decent supply of wine and cookies to get me through the eleven-hour days.

Our regular customers turned the place into a bad sitcom. There was Aberdeen, a soft, round black man in his sixties who spoke with a muddy Oxford accent, always brought me presents, always called me a scoundrel, which I rather liked, and always had a story to tell about his encounters with modern history's most powerful men.

"Mr. Rockefeller took me aside, and he told me . . ."

There was the satanist friend of Denny's, who would hang around and gab, using some of the ugliest racist terms I'd ever heard. I had dealt with members of the Klan before, I had dealt with neo-Nazis and members of the Posse Comitatus, but never had I heard any of them make reference to "complete extermination."

Every day presented me with a parade of the worst humanity had to offer. It was good fodder for the things I was writing for thirty-five dollars a week. I would hand in a piece to Derek, then wait a few days to see if he'd accept it or not. Soon he accepted whatever I submitted, and turned them into a weekly column, which I called "Slackjaw." The nickname had been following me around since the night Grinch chucked me under the chin in the Rathskeller.

For the first few months I wrote mostly music reviews and weekly rants that tried very hard to hurt everyone's feelings, schizophrenics included. Later I wrote about books, art shows, restaurants, but as time passed I was writing more about myself than about the things I was supposed to be reviewing. That was unfair, I thought, so I stopped talking about other people and things altogether, and just told stories about the adventures I'd gotten into that week.

Those early stories are embarrassing, a hackneyed mishmash of obvious stylistic influences and cheap histrionics.

A PLEA FOR VIOLENCE AND DEATH

Hey, I'm no different from anybody else. For the last few months, I've been havin' some of those Bad Thoughts sloshin' through my head. I find myself, as I'm sure all of us have at one time or another, wandering down the street, muttering things out loud like "Gonna kill all of you, each and every last one of you miserable pigfuckers. Gonna *kill* you, gonna sodomize your corpses, gonna dump you all in the sewer and set your filthy, stinking bodies on fire, gonna tie all of you bloated, rotting scum up in barbed wire, gonna . . ." Well, you get the picture. Not a pretty sight. . . .

Indeed. Perhaps even more embarrassing than the stories themselves was the fact that they really did upset people, and on a regular basis. The first piece of mail I received, in response to the first story I'd published, was a scrawled death threat from a man who was set to track me down with his dog and his gun and blow my "garbage head" off. My would-be killer went on to call me a "foul-mouthed crepe"—something I vowed to put on the menu should I ever have my own restaurant.

After writing a column in favor of heavy metal violence, I received a dense, poorly typed death threat at my home address. This was a troubling development. All the other angry mail was sent to the paper. The writer went to great lengths to describe the events surrounding the projected murder, rather than the murder itself. "Raise an unopened bottle of beer to your lips," he wrote, "to rehearse what it will feel like when I shove the gun in your mouth." He pointed out that by praising random acts of murder, as I had done, I forgot that I was as much a target as anyone else. This made perfect sense. In the last line, he informed me he would give me two more weeks to live. It was a smart move on his part. Had he been threatening someone normal, he would've caused the person two weeks of panic and bowel trouble. I was frustrated that he was making me wait that long.

The one problem I had with these circumstances was Laura. She should know about them, in case something did happen to me, but more important, to keep an eye out for herself. I didn't care what happened to me, but I didn't want her to get hurt. Laura read my stories and didn't much like them. She knew they were going to get me into trouble one day. If I showed her the letter, she'd flip. I knew she'd flip. That wouldn't help anything. I decided to wait out the two weeks and then show her the letter.

I went about my routine and almost forgot about the death threat. Though there had been such threats before, the ferocity of this letter nagged at me—maybe someone meant it this time.

On the night that marked the end of my two weeks, the night I was supposed to meet my demise at the hands of a clever psychopath who couldn't type very well, I showed Laura the letter. She didn't exactly panic, but she wasn't very happy. Eventually, over a couple of bottles of wine, I convinced her that the threat was over, that it was a joke, just somebody's idea of, well . . . something.

It was right about then that someone kicked in the front door to the building.

You had to go through two doors, with two different locks, in order to enter the building proper. Getting through the first door was not a big deal. I'd kicked it open on many an occasion myself, just to be manly. Then I'd pull out my keys and open the second door.

But whoever had kicked in the front door now did not have keys for the inner door, and started pounding on it. Pounding and kicking on that door something *fierce*—nothing polite about this request for entry. There were a lot of crazies in the neighborhood and we usually had to step over one or two of them to get out in the mornings, but this was something, someone, else. Someone with something important in mind, quite possibly my murder, held back by only a flimsy piece of wood a mere twenty feet from our apartment door.

Laura was already on edge after our talk, and now there seemed no question who was pounding on the door or what he wanted.

"James, what have you gotten yourself into this time?"

"It's okay. It'll take him a while to get through the door, as long as nobody lets him in. What we need is a plan."

We scoured the apartment for any weapons we could find, piled them on the chair next to the front door, and crouched there, whispering to each other. We each had a set of brass knuckles and a big butcher knife. We had a hatchet. We had a fish club (a kind of mini–baseball bat for knocking fish unconscious, I guess). We had a hammer. And though I'm not sure why, we had an air horn and a baggie full of extremely potent chili powder.

I laid out the plan as the pounding continued down the hall. "We kill the lights. I'm not sure how he'll be armed. When he gets to the apartment, we'll whip the door open, then you blast the air horn to startle him, and I'll throw the chili powder in his eyes. I'll whack him in the head with the club, and you get him in the jaw with your knucks. We should be able to drag him into the apartment. Then we'll slam the door and kill him. Just stab him to death."

It seemed like a good plan to both of us, but we were both a little drunk. The banging in the hallway was getting more frantic. We stayed crouched by the door, the two of us, a mighty team of vengeful sots, ready to dole out justice the way it was meant to be dealt. As George Wallace's assailant Arthur Bremer succinctly put it, "Irony abounds."

After forty-five minutes of banging and pounding and rattling of the doorknob down the hall, something finally gave way. Whether it was the lock or the door itself, we couldn't tell. Another punch or two and something fell loose and rattled on the floor. This was it.

Laura's grip tightened around the air horn; I readied the baggie full of chili powder. We couldn't see what was happening outside the apartment; we knew only that in a few short minutes, somebody was going to be dead. The question was who.

We heard the door swing open, and we both caught our breath. The footsteps approached from down the hall, accompanied by quiet muttering but no other noise. Our lights were out, the stereo was off, the cats were locked in the back room. It was just us against him now. I took hold of the doorknob but didn't dare turn it.

We heard someone slowly climb the three steps to our door. We were sweating, tense pumas poised to attack and kill without fear and without mercy. You could smell the bloodlust rising from our bodies.

I tried to think of something dramatic to say, something to make it seem even more like a grade-B revenge film, but nothing came.

Then we heard the footsteps turn and go upstairs. One flight. Two. Then a polite knock. A door opened, warm greetings were exchanged, the door closed, and everything was silent. It was the piano teacher who lived upstairs. He must have forgotten his keys.

I looked at the air horn and chili powder, then at Laura, before asking:

"Just what in the hell were we thinking?"

i've gotta be me

TROUBLE WAS TRACKING ME DOWN.

It was 1988. We had been in Philadelphia for more than a year now, and something was going very wrong. The hatred and rage that I had put on paper every week in my newspaper column were coming out of me when I was at home alone with Laura.

These feelings could be triggered by anything, no matter how slight—a trivial rejection, an encounter with bad ideas, the sound of a knife clattering into a sink, my banging my head on a bathroom cabinet. It always ended up the same way: with hands trembling, fists clenching and unclenching uncontrollably, head shaking, eyes narrowed, jaw grinding open and shut, hissing, growls erupting from my throat.

Laura was scared. I never raised a hand toward her, but there were moments when it seemed I might. Though I might be able to identify the source of the rage in each case, those sources were so diffuse that all they did was add up to the realization that something was going wrong. At first it was happening a few times a week; soon it was happening a few times a day, each spell lasting a half-hour or more.

I made an appointment with a doctor, and after several visits she farmed me out to specialists. "If they can't find anything," she said, "you might consider going to a psychiatrist."

"What about demonic possession?" I asked. That seemed to me the only logical explanation. I even had Laura believing. "Is that an option?"

"No, it's not."

The other doctors had their own answers as to what was causing the rage. One told me that it was hyperventilation and that I should breathe into a paper bag whenever I felt an attack coming on. Another said that it was low blood sugar and advised that I carry food with me to snack on throughout the day.

After weeks of testing, the tantrums still cropping up four, five, six times a day, a neurologist, my last hope before turning to a shrink or an exorcist, concluded that the problem was nestled deep in the vacant crevices of my brain. He scheduled me for an EEG, a simple test that, true to form, I failed.

The first rule of the game was that I had to wake up at three in the morning the day of the test. Not, as I had thought beforehand, because the doctor wanted me to shake the funny sleepy-time patterns out of my brain, but instead to make sure the funny sleepy-time patterns were still there. These give a more accurate reading of what goes on in the brain, the neurologist told me.

I got up at three, made an omelet, and watched *Vertigo* on television. After the movie, it was still early, so I listened to a Steve Lawrence album. I arrived at the hospital in plenty of time, mazed my way up elevators and around floors until I found the appointed room, where I filled out forms and waited. When my number came up, a young nurse took me to a room with a desk, a chair, a hospital bed, and a wallful of high-tech gadgetry.

She sat me in a chair, whipped out a red wax pencil and a plastic tape measure, and proceeded to mark X's on twenty-five precise points on my skull, earlobes, forehead, and temples, and deep under my mess of matted hair. That done, she steered me to the bed, had me lie down, pulled out a blunt-tipped emery-board pencil, and scraped each of those twenty-five X's clean. Then she pulled out a glue gun and a dentist's spit-sucking tube that worked in reverse. She dolloped out glue on each X spot, attached an electrical contact, and blew the glue dry with a mixture of air and ether that exploded from the tube in a loud hiss. She poked an electrode through each contact until the surface of the flesh was just pierced.

Now I lay there, twenty-five wires spiraling from my head, and she still wasn't finished. She pulled out two longer electrodes and shoved the first one up my left nostril.

"You know, I've only done this once before. We've been really short-staffed here for the past month, and they just asked me if I'd do it when I came in this morning."

"Oh?" My eyes widened and began to water.

"My, this certainly is a *narrow* nasal passage!" She chortled as she poked the wire home to the underside of my brain. "The other one shouldn't be as uncomfortable. If one nasal passage is really narrow, the other is much wider."

And it was, I suppose. But that brought along its own problems. With both wires tickling my brain, every swallow sent the loose one in the right nostril twitching and jumping, poking where it shouldn't, messing up the readings she was trying to take. But at least she was finished hooking me up.

She went to the foot of the electric bed, pulled it from the wall, and reached down and unplugged it. "These things leak so much electricity. You wouldn't believe how many people get electrocuted by hospital beds every year."

"Really."

She took a seat in front of the wall of machinery and flicked a switch.

Bzzzzzzgggrrrrrmmmbzzz . . .

"Now go to sleep," she ordered.

Right. A nest of foreign and wicked electrical current was wrapped around my head, I had two wires shoved up my nose, and a machine was hissing and buzzing not three feet from me.

And to top things off, Steve Lawrence singing "I've Gotta Be Me" had been in my head all morning, and it showed no signs of leaving now.

I tried to sleep, and almost made it there a few times, too, except that whenever I was about to drop off, she would lean over and ask, "Are you asleep yet?"

"Not anymore."

"Well, I'm watching the patterns here, and you keep drifting off, but then you wake up again."

"That's because you keep asking me questions."

She had a better idea. She maneuvered a lamp in front of me and flashed a strobe light into my eyes, thinking it might hypnotize me. While it didn't hypnotize me, it did give me a grating headache.

I had wires up my nose, I had a headache, Steve Lawrence was starting his hundred-sixteenth encore, and my technician friend was annoyed that I wasn't falling asleep.

"Are you at all sleepy?"

"I was before I came in here."

After forty-five minutes she gave up and, with a twist of disgust on her lips, jerked the wires off my head and out of my nose and scrubbed the glue from my hair with a foul-smelling substance even thicker and stickier than the glue.

I lifted myself from the bed and slammed my hat down tight. With that stuff in my hair I figured I might never get the hat off again, but that was okay. I rarely took it off as it was.

I left. Failed again.

The doctor who had put me up to the joke in the first place called with the results a few days later.

"There's one funny wave here, in the section of the brain that causes certain funny emotions like rage."

"I'm glad this is all amusing you."

"But this might be the key into what's been causing your problems."

"I think I might be able to tell you where that funny wave comes from," I offered. "Are you familiar with Steve Lawrence?"

Two weeks, a CAT scan, and an MRI later, the same neurologist was able to point to something on a picture.

"There it is," he said proudly.

And there it was, indeed, a black smudge on the left temporal lobe of my brain.

"That's scar tissue," he said, "right at the locus of strange emotions like rage. What you have is a form of epilepsy that expresses itself in what we call 'rage seizures.'"

"What's next? Lobotomy?" It seemed like a good idea.

"Oh no. No, no, no . . ." He sounded as if he had suddenly considered it, and decided that a lobotomy wasn't such a bad idea.

"What then?" I asked after a pause.

"We can try some drugs that will probably control it." The lobotomy idea was sounding better and better to him, it seemed.

He gave me a prescription for an anticonvulsant called Tegretol and sent me on my way. It took a few weeks for the drug to take hold, but once it did, the seizures began to fade. Not completely, but I could try to resume something resembling a normal life.

BY THEIR VERY NATURE, used-book stores attract a string of regulars who, once a week, once a month, bring in a boxful of old books they want to sell. It's an easy way to make a couple of bucks. Not much, mind you, but enough to buy maybe a sandwich and a beer someplace. At Denny's shop, most of these were normal people, who were either cleaning out their own libraries or clearing what had been left on the curb by others, who had given up the habit. Rarely did they show up with anything worthwhile or interesting. Books without covers, books covered in mold, Italian travel guides from 1956, old Boy Scout manuals. Piles of nothing, which we could never sell. To them it didn't matter: they'd happily return the next week or month, whether or not we bought anything from them, carrying another box full of crap.

But there were other types, too.

I was at the shop one Tuesday, slow as usual—nobody's much interested in books on Tuesdays—when an old man appeared at the counter.

"I'm told you boys buy books," he said.

"You're told right. If it's worth our while."

He set his bag on the ground and reached inside, slowly—old man he was—and pulled out three copies of Albert Goldman's John Lennon biography, which was causing quite a stir at the time. He dropped them on the counter.

"How much I get for these?"

They were brand-new, pristine—how could they be anything else? The book had been out only a few weeks.

I looked at the books, then back at the old man. He reminded me of Grady from *Sanford and Son*—or maybe Dick Gregory—a skeleton in a tattered raincoat, gray ragged shirt beneath it, soiled brown pants, white beard, rumpled hat over a wide forehead. He didn't look—and granted, I was making assumptions here—like much of a reader. He definitely didn't look like a man who would have received three copies of the Lennon biography for his birthday.

That was cool, though; I'd bite. We had regular dealings with book thieves, too. They usually showed up once, were disappointed with the money, and never came back; they did leave some good material.

"Six bucks," I told the man.

"Six each."

"No, six total."

He slapped the top book, his palm coming down hard on Lennon's face. "But these are brand-new books!"

"It's pretty obvious that they're brand-new," I said. "Nobody owns three copies of . . . well, not by accident."

We eyed each other. He was a desperate old man.

"Look," I said finally, "I don't want to know where these came from. I'll give you ten dollars—which is a helluva lot more than anyone else in town'll give you—and that's that. That's the end of it, okay?"

"Yeah . . . yeah." He put out his hand. I counted ten singles and laid them in his palm. I set the books behind the counter, turned around to thank him, but he was gone.

I priced the first book and put it on a table. The other two I kept behind the counter. No point in raising suspicions. By the end of the day, all three had been sold.

The next morning about eleven, he appeared at the counter again, another shopping bag in hand.

"I got some more books for you," he said, happily.

Shit. I could see that I had gotten myself into something I shouldn't have. *Whatever happens, this is going to end badly.*

He reached into his bag and pulled out another little pile. Two copies of *The Satanic Verses*, three other titles from the bestseller list. Useless, but glossy. People'd buy them.

I scratched the back of my head and winced. "These are real nice," I told him, "but I dunno. . . ."

"Damn right they're nice. Bestsellers! Look at 'em!"

"Look, sir—what's your name, anyway?"

"Son, you can just call me Mr. Shakeybones."

Oh, Jesus Christ. This was becoming an exercise in foolishness. "Slackjaw Meets Mr. Shakeybones." Like another Marvel Comics Super Team-Up Special.

I stuck out my hand. "Well, Mr. Shakeybones, my name's Jim." We shook. His dark hand was rough but frail.

"Now, let me explain something to you. I got no problem with your taking these books from wherever you're taking them from. But having them here in the store makes me an accessory, see? If you're ever nabbed, I'm liable, too, understand? I got no time for that."

He smiled, proud of himself. "Ain't never been nabbed yet—and I'm an old man."

"Uh-huh." I looked at the books again. "Jesus. Okay. We'll do it again, just this once. But no more. From now on, I have no idea who you are." He nodded and held out his hand. I gave him twelve dollars, and he vanished again.

Later that afternoon, Denny stopped by. He made his usual spin through the inventory, and stopped when he came to the new copy of *The Satanic Verses*. He plucked it off the shelf and brought it over.

"Where did this come from?"

I pretended to be busy, and gave the book the briefest of glances. "Oh, some guy came in to sell it today."

"Well, who?"

"I didn't ask his name. I'd never seen him before." What was I supposed to say? Oh, just some book thief, name of Mr. Shakeybones?

Denny cracked the book open and flipped through it.

"This is a new book."

"Guess it is."

"How much'd you give him for it?"

"Just a couple bucks. He took it and left happy."

I was in for it. Some lecture about buying stolen property,

some shit about the bookseller's code of ethics. But instead, a strange look came over Denny's face.

"So what do you suppose, these fell off a truck?"

I was seeing evidence of the combination of Denny's avowed communist leanings and the greedy streak required to run a business. His communist side loved the idea of stealing from B. Dalton and Barnes & Noble, his greedy side knew that he could sell these books for more than most of the other garbage we had on the tables and shelves. Plus, if we had regular access to new books, big new bestsellers, more people would visit our stand.

"I have no idea," I continued to fib. "He brought this in, then he split."

Denny gave me a strange look but didn't say anything.

It was a strange position to be in. I had been an active book thief in Madison and Minneapolis. I knew how easy it was. About half my library consisted of books I had lifted. But I always stole books to read, not to sell. Now here I was, feeling queasy about being a fence for a brother-in-arms. I was growing old.

Despite what I'd told him the day before, on Thursday morning Mr. Shakeybones was back, with an even bigger bagful. I looked through the books. He obviously didn't know what he had—he must have been blindly lifting things off the front display tables of whatever bookstore he was hitting.

I counted out the bills into his open palm. "Okay now," I said, "if we're going to have an arrangement, you gotta keep the quality up on your end. You can't start bringing me crap and still expect to get paid."

"So tell me what you want. Gimme a list or something."

I pulled out a pad of paper. Then I thought better. Why give this man something with my handwriting on it to carry around in his pocket and refer to as he filled up his shopping bag? No. I wasn't going to give him any incriminating evidence to hand over to the cops.

"Howsabout I give you some ideas to keep in your head while you make your rounds? We want good stuff, like the stuff you brought in yesterday and the day before. Stuff off the bestseller tables, sure, but no crap. Got no use for crap. And Elvis books. Elvis books are always good." That last bit was for me: I figured I should get something out of this, too.

And so for a few weeks we had a good thing going. Mr. Shakeybones would stop by a few times a week with his bag, we'd chat, he'd tell me where he had gotten his books (a B. Dalton four blocks away), I'd give him five dollars a book, he'd disappear, and most everything he brought in would be sold by the end of the day at a huge mark-up. But one day, as everything does, something changed. Mr. Shakeybones brought in his bag and I paid him off. Instead of disappearing immediately as he usually did, though, he kept standing by the counter as I priced the new pile he'd brought in.

"What's up?" I asked.

"I want more money."

I guess I should have known this would happen, eventually.

"Can't do it. We're paying you more per book than we pay anyone—than we've *ever* paid anyone."

"Yeah, well, I'm the one who's taking the risk. I'm the one who's doing all the work—"

"And that's why we're paying you more than anyone else." I was starting to get pissed. "If you're scared of the work, then stop. If you don't like the money, take your books someplace else."

"We had a deal, son—"

"And I'm sticking to that deal."

"I go down, you all go down with me." He hissed, turned on his heels, and left.

Well, that was it. I wasn't going to let some old junkie thief threaten me. I pulled out the phone book and looked up the number of the B. Dalton he'd been hitting. I'd never been a rat, and I didn't want to turn into one. The idea of honor among thieves is a myth, anyway. Man threatens me, regardless of his station in life, his level of desperation, and my first impulse— granted, not always the best—is to destroy him.

I dialed the bookstore.

The next morning I sat behind the counter, sweating. It was another slow day. At about one—I'd just finished my lunch and was glancing around wearily—I saw him coming. Pretty fast for an old man. Still in his smelly raincoat and rumpled hat, his eyes wild. He was out of breath and sweating worse than I was.

"What the hell happened to you?" I asked when he reached the counter, even though I had some notion.

"They almost caught me, son. This bitch came around the corner while I was at my work and let out a yell. That little *bitch*—" He took a few breaths. "But they didn't catch me, I was too fast for them."

"Good for you."

"I didn't get nothin' today, though."

"That's no big deal. You'll get something tomorrow."

"It looks like I lost my source. They didn't catch me, but they sure as hell saw me."

"You'll deal," I said. "So why are you here, anyway, if you don't have anything for me?"

"I need some money, son. Just a little bit."

"But you didn't bring me anything, so I don't owe you anything. This is a business deal we had."

"Aw, c'mon, son—I just need a few bucks." He was fidgeting, moving, from one foot to the other, maybe from fright, maybe from need.

"Can't do it. I'm real sorry." I was the one in control. This was a place I'd never been.

"Come on, son—just a couple little bucks."

"No."

"Shit, son." He turned and walked away, but a few minutes later he was back.

"Son, *please*. I ain't never done you wrong, please, just this once—"

"*Christ* Almighty," I spat. I reached into my pocket and pulled out a five, and slapped it into his hand. He looked at the bill.

"Is that all? Hey, I need more than that—"

That was it. Offer a man an unnecessary kindness and have him expect more. Nothing irks me more. I pointed nowhere in particular, but away from me. "*Get . . . the hell . . . outta here!*"

The few customers at the stand turned and looked.

Mr. Shakeybones vanished, and I tried to tell myself that he had let me down, knowing full well that I had let myself down. For a moment I had had some power, and in that same moment I had become a rat.

I never saw Mr. Shakeybones again.

In the next weeks it was increasingly apparent that the book-store was in trouble. Mail and bills were stacking up behind the counter, and the stock on the shelves was growing thinner and less attractive. The Reading Terminal's landlord informed me that Denny hadn't paid the rent in six months. Denny came to the store less and less often; he would phone me two or three mornings a week and ask if I could work for him. Then he stopped coming in altogether, leaving me to run the place twelve hours a day, seven days a week.

"I just can't come in," he'd say feebly from home, "I go into a complete panic." To prove his point on a day he did come in, he began to shake and sweat a few minutes after stepping behind the counter, and I had to get the fellow from the wine shop to watch the place while I walked Denny to his van.

The piles of paperwork in the way and angry phone calls about Denny's unpaid bills were exhausting me. I wouldn't be able to do this much longer, not seven days a week. One day I begged him to come in—if only to take the paperwork away and handle it at home.

A week later he showed up with his mother. It was about eleven on a Saturday morning, and the market was packed, as it always was on the weekends. I'd been there since eight. Half an hour after his arrival, Denny was curled up in fetal position in a folding chair in a corner, shaking like a frightened puppy. I gathered his papers and mail, handed the pile to him, and told his mother to take him home. Two weeks later, the stand shut down. Denny drove up early on a Saturday morning, and quietly and furiously he and I boxed up the remaining stock and packed it in the van. Denny drove away and never looked back.

I WAS JOBLESS AGAIN, and scraping to get by with Laura on her graduate fellowship money. The two of us started fighting more, and now the fights weren't the result of my seizures; they were about fundamentals, like attitudes and money and failure. We didn't need any more bad news.

I should have known better than to think such a thing. The week Laura and I decided—despite everything and against all sense—to get married, I had an eye appointment at Wills Eye Hospital. Just a routine yearly checkup. The ophthalmologist who examined me—a man I had never seen before—told me that I'd be completely blind within a few years, probably by the time I was thirty-five. He explained to me for the first time what retinitis pigmentosa was, and what it implied. For all the eye doctors I had seen since I was three years old, not one of them had told me that I was actually going *blind*. I had heard the schoolyard rumors, and there was that encounter with Uncle Tom, but I had ignored everything, dismissing it as simple morbid speculation. Now science had confirmed that those childhood rumors were true, and that there was no escape.

A few days after that news, I got a phone call from Grinch, who informed me he was moving to town. The blindness I could handle. That was some time away, I'd deal with it when I got there. But Grinch's moving to Philly was another matter completely. The problem was an ancient one. I think even Aeschylus wrote a play about it: Fiancée doesn't like your wild friends. It was the stuff of the worst television. Mayhem and laughter ensue. Everything works out in the end. Except in this case, there was Grinch. Television sitcoms had never dealt with anyone like Grinch.

kicking a
gift horse

SIX MONTHS AFTER the book stand closed, I found work
as a bill collector in West Philly. I was still writing "Slackjaw" for
the *Welcomat*, but that was bringing in only a pittance. Collecting
bills, I wasn't making as much as I had at the bookstall, there were
no tills I could tap in this place, and I had to buy my own wine, but
it was something. And Grinch had moved to town.

As a consequence of his near-demonic presence, Laura and I
had postponed our wedding, and tensions between us were
higher than ever. Despite medication, my seizures were assailing
me and making things only that much worse. My eyesight, too,
continued to deteriorate, but slowly enough that I could choose
to ignore it. What had the ophthalmologist said? Five years? Ten
years? Ten years was a lifetime.

The office I was working in was across the street from an old
bar, the Shamrock Pub. There were three or four bars on the
block, but the Shamrock was my favorite. It was simple, it was
well lit, a rugged old Irish bar.

I would go in, sit at the end of the bar close to the door, drink
my three beers, and leave. Never said anything to anybody.
Nobody in there ever said anything to anybody. It was an aging
crowd, mostly men who'd been drinking there every day for
years. The clientele was evenly split between black and white.
And it was a beer crowd. Once you decided to move on to gin or
vodka, you went across the street to the Cherry Tree.

One day as I sat in the Shamrock, I noticed a crumbling, wasted black whore I'd never seen there before, though she seemed like another regular.

"Hey, John Denver!" she shouted from five stools down. I looked at the other faces down the bar before determining she was talking to me.

"Hey, John Denver!" she shouted again, raising her bottle in a toast. I raised mine, and we both took a drink. I went back to minding my own business.

A few minutes later she shouted again. "Hey, John Denver!" She bared her crooked, broken yellow teeth in a big smile, and we raised our bottles a second time in honor of the great John Denver.

It unnerved me to have attention called to myself in public. Maybe she was looking for a trick, or trying to set me up for something bad. I'd become more than a little paranoid about the motivations of strangers lately. But after the fifth or sixth toast, I understood. She was just being friendly. She liked John Denver, thought I resembled John Denver, and was toasting that. I sat back and accepted her friendliness.

Grinch, who had moved to an apartment in the neighborhood, started meeting me at the Shamrock for lunch. Despite Laura's apprehension, he and I didn't see each other all that often. We would go to a punk show at the Khyber Pass or ride out to the Philadelphia Park racetrack for an afternoon now and then, but that was about it. We smashed no windows and set no fires.

When he roared into town on his stripped-down Harley-Davidson, a set of steer horns nailed to the handlebars, he had been hoping we would get the Pain Amplifiers back together. I knew that was not going to happen, if only because we had thrown our instruments away, and Sears, Roebuck was not about to offer him another credit card.

We began spending a few hours every day at the Shamrock, old-man style, talking about what might have been, making big plans that both of us knew would never come to pass. Grinch didn't have a job yet, and mine was inconsequential.

One Monday, as usual, Grinch and I were downing our lunchtime Buds, chomping on beer nuts, and smoking up a toxic cloud, as we condemned the world and laughed about our schemes to bring on the apocalypse. I didn't know it then, but he was gearing himself up to tell me that, after four months in town, he was moving back to Chicago. Things hadn't worked out in Philly, or more specifically, *I* hadn't worked out. Before he had his chance to tell me this, though, voices at the other end of the bar rose and confronted each other in the kind of rage you don't recognize as rage until it's almost over.

Renee, the day bartender, screamed, "I can't take this fuckin' shit no more!" and stomped out from behind the bar. Bob, an eighty-seven-year-old newly widowed barfly, had stepped over beyond her guff line.

Before she left, Renee stopped and said to me, "You write one word about this, and I'll knock ya on yer ass."

Grinch and I gave her our most heartfelt innocent looks.

Jeannie, Renee's twin and owner of the Shamrock, turned to Grinch and me after her sister had slammed out the door.

"You guys need some work?"

Grinch and I looked at each other, then over our empties at her.

"Sure, why the hell not?"

We were always needing some work. Besides, after spending as much time on the paying sides of bars as we had, we knew the crossover couldn't be that hard. Grinch decided that maybe he'd stick around awhile, anyway.

When we met up on my lunch break the next day, the stakes

were upped. Not only was Jeannie looking for bartenders, she was divining for young blood to breathe some new life and capital into the place. She was a twenty-year veteran and was worn and tired of the feed-the-drunks game. She wanted to move to Florida to be near her children, and she was ready to hand the place over to someone else.

It was too perfect. Control over the jukebox, VCR, redecoration, clientele. During lunch Grinch and I talked about the bands who would play at the grand reopening party. We were going to dredge up the meanest, strangest, sickest crowd Philadelphia had seen in a long, long time in one place, with freak nights, arm wrestling, drink specials for mental patients, a jukebox full of bad music.

"A place needs a gimmick to make it nowadays," Jeannie urged us.

"Hell"—Grinch clapped a meaty claw on my shoulder—"gimmick is our middle name!"

I took the next day off from work, and Grinch and I arrived at the bar with bags of festoonery to begin the restoration. The first thing up was a three-part wooden Mexican ceremonial mask. A leering face with a protruding tongue, an angry goat's head, and an overdecorated cat monster stared from the wall: this is what people would see when they walked in. After that we put up exploitation-movie posters, a hundred-strong collection of the world's sickest postcards, a lot of Elvis, the set of steer horns from Grinch's Harley, and a peculiar German religious document Grinch had picked up somewhere. None of it made much sense. Semantic interference works best in a nonpolitical context. And it works especially well on drunkards.

Jeannie couldn't have been happier. We had worried that she would be offended by some of our plans, but she seemed excited about everything. Everything was great. Everything was *perfect*.

In the back of my mind I began to worry about what we were letting ourselves get sucked into. Jeannie didn't know a damn thing about us, and neither of us had any bartending experience—yet here she was, handing us the Shamrock on a silver platter. We didn't know a thing about her, and we took it.

As the decorating and planning went on, I stopped thinking and went along. I didn't tell Laura that I'd been given a bar to run. I'd do that later. Grinch and I got "Black Betty" and "If I Can Dream" and some Metallica and Conway Twitty for the jukebox, to complement the collection of awfulness we had acquired independently over the years, and prepared some ads and fliers.

On our first day of official bartender training, Jeannie called us to the back door and whispered nervously: "I'm just warning ya. You're facing some mighty stiff opposition here. They loved Renee. Did you hear what they were saying about cults back there? They think you're devil worshippers or something. But if we just hang in there, we'll win 'em over." She gave our arms a maternal squeeze, to let us know she was behind us. We trusted her.

Grinch and I had faced stiff opposition before, but the dim lights of the Shamrock could not conceal the hot-coal stares we got when we stepped behind the bar.

We survived two days and nights, determined to win over those poor, drunken, unemployed louts if it killed us. Eddie, the weekend bartender, came in on Saturday, so we had some time to plan for our complete takeover the following week. Early Sunday morning, Grinch got a frantic message from Jeannie, asking him to call her back immediately.

Things at the Shamrock had gotten uglier than usual on Saturday night. Even uglier than we were planning. The regular crowd, not big to begin with, had had enough of weird carvings, postcard images of congenitally deformed hands and gunshot

wounds, threats to their Anita Baker and Dire Straits on the jukebox. And they decided to put an end to it.

Those fine, decent churchgoing souses, with their pock-
marked, swollen faces, rose together, a single, hot tribal scream
boiling in their wormy guts, and they set to destroying the
Shamrock. They smashed the mask, tore posters and postcards
off the walls, hooted with destructive glee. Then they set the
place on fire and ran away, howling into the night.

Jeannie wasn't so sure anymore that we should take over her
bar. Or what was left of it.

The dream of a couple of power mad, perversity-driven
young sots had lasted for almost a week. It was not the worst thing
to have it go up in smoke, and it did make a certain sense. I
didn't blame the old drunks for torching the place if that was what
it took to prevent devil worshippers from taking over. I was more
than relieved, actually. Once I had agreed to take part, I was
afraid to tell anyone that I couldn't see a goddamn thing behind
that bar. Bright as it was, it wasn't nearly bright enough for me to
function.

A week later, Grinch got on his bike and rode back to Chicago.
I should have known things with Grinch would end in fire.

With his departure, Laura and I resumed planning our wedding. We'd set a date and a place. Laura, who was studying lin-
guistics and speech perception, and spent any free moments
writing graceful, beautiful poems, and hard-edged avant-garde
plays, was also a bit of an architectural historian, so we were going
to fly to Chicago, to be married in Frank Lloyd Wright's Unity
Temple.

Then we were going to move to New York.

I had vowed I would never move to New York. Never. It
seemed so damn common. Everybody moved to New York. But
the faculty at the City University of New York was encouraging

Laura to transfer there to finish her Ph.D. It was where she wanted to be.

As she talked about these plans, I grinned a strained grin. She had no idea that I couldn't do it, couldn't go up there. Not with my eyesight disappearing the way it was. I was scared of New York, of encroaching blindness, and of the combination of the two. Thing was, I was too proud. I couldn't, and wouldn't, admit my fears to anyone. Not even myself.

We were married in Chicago on June 1, 1991. In July, we moved to Brooklyn.

square pegs in
a round museum

IT MUST HAVE SEEMED like a good idea when we were drunk.

Laura and I decided to go to Times Square on New Year's Eve. Having lived in town for only a few months, we were still more tourists pushing our limits than we were New Yorkers. We wanted free entertainment. We wanted to take our minds off the facts that I was jobless again and we were barely making the rent for a cramped Brooklyn apartment, complete with two cats and too many books.

At nine we got on an F train in Brooklyn, bound for Forty-second Street in Manhattan. A group of drunken high schoolers swung around the poles and danced on the orange plastic seats at the other end of the car. There was nobody else in the car. Laura and I were obvious targets.

One of the kids, a skinny guy in a leather jacket and a card-board hat, wobbled his way over and leaned in close. "I'll give you twenty dollars if you're carrying a Rolling Stones album." He laughed at his funny joke.

I kept looking at his fancy sneakers, my fedora shading my eyes.

"Well? Ya got one?"

I let my glare meet his. "Get the fuck away from me or I'll plant a shiv in your ribs." I guess I looked as though I might have been carrying. The kid went away to whisper to his pals.

When the train reached the Stop of Doom, Laura and I got

out. Aboveground, the corner of Forty-second and Sixth Avenue was a madhouse. It looked as if a riot were taking place, but if it was, it was a riot at half speed. There were no windows being smashed, no cars upended and burning. Just too many people packing the street, being prodded along by cops in riot gear.

Sixth Avenue was blocked off, so we fell in with the slow-moving horde, including the jackasses with their noisemakers, and shambled past Broadway, toward Seventh. Cops were stopping random celebrants and patting them down. Every other one had a bottle—champagne, whiskey, vodka. It may have been New Year's, but liquor on the streets was still against the law. The cops opened and emptied bottles into the gutter before horrified eyes.

When we reached Seventh Avenue, we found it cordoned off, too, with barricades and a line of police. Clubs at the ready, they nudged everyone on to Eighth.

Despite the bright lights, I couldn't see well. I had no idea where we were going, where we were being sent. It seemed entirely plausible that the police were going to march us into a warehouse on Tenth and lock the doors and torch the place. But by now there was no question of turning back. Trying to shove our way against the tide would have been foolish. I hung tight to Laura's arm as she pulled me along.

The mob turned north on Eighth. Cross streets were blocked off, so we had to remain on the avenue. More blue police barricades, more cops eager for trouble. Every few blocks, a cop would pull a barricade aside and let five or six people slip through. Laura and I were witnessing a study in brilliant low-tech crowd control.

Somewhere in the mid-sixties, we were in the right place when the barricades were moved aside and we could sniggle through. We were told to keep walking, not to stop, not to look around, until we reached Broadway. Not wanting to be shot in the back, we followed orders.

On television, New Year's Eve in Times Square looks like a freewheeling, nonstop dance party, a fluid mass of people bumping randomly about. It was anything but. Each block had been transformed into a cattle pen. There Laura and I stood, cold, shivering, stuck in a makeshift jail between Sixty-second and Sixty-third streets with maybe two hundred other partyers. It was almost a quarter to eleven and I couldn't even see the goddamn ball, twenty blocks to the south.

Clearly, this was not something Laura and I were interested in doing anymore. We had had enough of the communal celebration of an arbitrary date.

Leaving ought to have been simple. We were out of the stream of moving people; all we had to do was slip under the barricade and go back to the subway. You would think the cops would be happy to see us leaving: it meant two fewer people for them to keep an eye on. The moment I started to crawl out, though, the cops were on top of me.

"Get back in there!"

"I just want to go home now."

"You can't do that."

"I . . . *can't?*"

Laura helped me up, then started plotting. She went to the corner of our pen and pushed it open. Since she was a woman, she figured, the cops would be nicer to her. Sometimes we were pretty dumb.

As she was trying to slip out, a short female cop ran over, planted her billy club in Laura's chest, and shoved her backward, into me.

"Don't you touch me," Laura growled. She has a look that

accompanies phrases like that—it's a killer, stops you dead in your tracks.

The cop pointed at some other, taller policeman a few yards away. "He's my supervisor. He told me to."

"Then why don't you tell your supervisor that we're just trying to go home? My husband is sick, and I have to get him out of here." I was feeling sick of humanity at the time, so Laura wasn't far from the truth.

There was new activity among the police at our intersection. Walkie-talkies were squawking, cops who had been standing around were suddenly in motion. The female cop came to where we were.

"Okay, you can leave," she told us.

"Thanks so much," Laura said.

"But you have to give us a few minutes to get set up here."

"What?"

"We have to create a corridor for you."

"What?"

"To get you out of here, we have to clear a path."

Laura and I looked at each other, then at the cop. "Okay."

"Now," she went on, "when I give you the word, you have to run. I mean *run,* down to that group of policemen on the next block. They'll tell you where to go from there."

It seemed like an elaborate practical joke by the NYPD to get back at citizens who wouldn't play along. Like those fake cops in Disneyland who arrest you for not having a good time. Still, we went along with it, confused, not knowing exactly what to expect or what else to do. Maybe they would have a special pen waiting just for us. Our cop muttered something into her radio, and someone muttered back.

"Okay," she told us, *"run!"*

We did. We were both in long coats, the streets were slippery

with ice and spilled champagne, but we ran, and we kept running. I stole a glance behind to see if anyone had a bead on us or
if they had released their dogs. Nothing. Laura dragged me
through the empty, frozen New Year's night toward something: a
group of ten policemen waiting for us at the end of the block.

They shuttled us through another barricade, none of them
saying a word, and suddenly we were on our own. We hurried
through the strangely empty, strangely well-lit streets to the nearest subway entrance and caught an empty train into Brooklyn.

By eleven forty-five we were in our apartment again, back in
the warmth, back with the cats, back in a place where we were
allowed to drink. We took off our coats and gloves and shoes and
opened a bottle of cheap champagne, and waited for our feet and
hands to thaw out. I turned on the television. There was Times
Square, with those thousands of tiny faces mashed together,
everyone having a fabulous time. Laura and I curled up on the
floor and watched. We were comfortable, we were sitting down,
and we were alone. At midnight we heard a muffled explosion
and looked out our window to see fireworks being shot off over
Prospect Park nearby. For tonight at least, things were okay, finally, especially with Laura plotting for me.

Some things, however, she couldn't plot me out of. Some
things, no amount of logic could help. For the next six months I
remained jobless. I mailed out résumés, and they vanished into
the ether. "New York's a tough town," I'd say. "Competition's
mighty fierce." But you can say that only so many times before
the sympathetic eye across the table begins to look resentful.

WHEN THE GUGGENHEIM MUSEUM REOPENED in
the summer of 1992 with a seven-story addition tacked on the
back, the museum's director, Thomas Krens, had an idea. Instead

of hiring the same rent-a-guards most other museums in New York were content with, the Gugg would go the European route and hire struggling artists to handle security. Not only would they care about protecting the Picassos and the Francis Bacon triptych, they would be able, at a moment's notice, to talk about the artwork to visitors, thereby easing the pressure on overworked tour guides.

I had my continuing weekly column at the *Welcomat,* but in the year or so since Laura and I had moved to Brooklyn, I'd been unable to drum up even a whiff or promise of work. I had been to a dozen job interviews, all disasters. I was lucky enough to be married to an amateur Frank Lloyd Wright scholar when the Guggenheim ad appeared in the paper. Laura filled me in on the building's history and gave me a few books to read so I could talk a good game at the interview.

When I was ushered into the interviewer's office, it was immediately apparent to me that she was blinder than I was. She took my résumé and held it nearly flush to her face, the way I used to do with books before my parents recognized there might be a problem. This gave me a potential opening: I could bring up my own failing eyesight to have an in with this woman, some common ground. Or should I stick with the architecture?

I stuck with the architecture. Most people weren't too eager to hire a blind man in New York. Especially to protect priceless works of art. A few days after the interview, the woman called me and told me I had the job.

The rest of the new guards were artists, mostly: painters, sculptors, architects, printmakers, writers, musicians, dancers, actors. Since struggling artists in New York are of a different breed from that of struggling artists in Milan or Geneva, the new crew also counted a smattering of junkies and potheads, an armload of drunks, an exiled Eastern European revolutionary, a religious fanatic or two, and a few people—including an ex–Navy man—who were unabashedly, openly insane. We were outfitted in matching Italian designer suits with big padded shoulders and ugly silk ties. *Boom,* instant subculture.

The job itself seemed very simple, but in reality was a killer: stand in one spot—given the design of the Guggenheim, usually on an incline—for ten hours a day, four days a week, and prevent visitors from getting too close to the artworks or taking photographs (the latter would reduce postcard sales in the gift shop).

Most folks who visit museums have no idea what the guards have to tolerate. This is what my fellow guards and I experienced, during a typical ten-hour day: Packs of wild grade-school children on a field trip, running roughshod over Giacometti sculptures. Tourists protesting, "But I am *French!*" when told not to touch the paintings. American visitors demanding their money back, arguing that there was no real art in the museum. Whining artists convinced we were there to serve them. And a museum administration, having soon recognized the folly of its decision to hire artists, doing everything in its power to get rid of us without bringing about a class-action suit.

Every morning before my shift, I would walk to the center of the ground floor and look up at the rotunda and the skylight. The Guggenheim is a remarkable building, a beautiful building, where every turn reveals a new trick, a clever play in Wright's design. Every morning I breathed in the beauty of my surroundings, and it carried me through most of the day. It was a hell of a lot better than working in a cubicle, even if I did have to deal with the public. With those walls around me, I could mostly ignore people, at least for a few hours.

Part of my job was to make sure that tourists didn't blow on the Calder mobiles on exhibit. When visitors asked why they weren't allowed to blow on them, I was supposed to explain that the collective spit from millions of people blowing on the artwork would coat the mobile, eat through the paint and the metal, and eventually reduce it to dust.

I was standing next to *Three Leaves and Four Petals,* saying things like, "Don't blow, please," and "Don't even think about blowing on that," when a rich old lady started giving me shit about not being able to see it move.

"Look, lady, just use your imagination," I told her. "It's not that hard."

She looked wistfully at the mobile. "Have you ever seen it move?" she asked.

"Yeah, I suppose I have."

"Oh, it must have been so *exciting!*"

"I suppose, if you're easily excited," I told her flatly.

Her eyes went narrow and gray. "Well, if you were an artist, you would realize how creative it was, and that in itself would be exciting." She smiled coldly, but didn't look at me.

All the guards dealt with such encounters in their own way. Some feigned no knowledge of English. Some turned draconian, maintaining a sense of order through thinly veiled threats of violence. Myself, I resorted to semantic interference. I gave people nonsense mixed with solid information in order to confuse and disarm them, and get them quickly away from me.

One evening during a big show by Lothar Baumgarten, a goofy German who was paid an absurd amount of money to have his crew of indentured assistants paint the names of New World Indian tribes along the inside of the spiral, I was approached by a group of Japanese tourists.

"Excuse me," their translator asked in hesitant English, "but can you tell us what this is all about?" She gestured to the names painted on the walls.

"Why, of course I can," I said, and snapped into helpful

knowledgeable-guard mode. "All these names you see along here are the names of popular American snack foods. Every American tries to eat one or more of these snack items every day, and this is just the Guggenheim and Mr. Baumgarten's way of celebrating a central part of our culture."

She nodded and smiled gratefully, turned to her group, and translated. When she was done, they all smiled, nodded, thanked me, and continued on their way. Shortly afterward, a memo was circulated informing us guards that we were no longer to discuss the artwork with the visitors; instead, we were allowed to inform them only when the next official tour was taking place.

Most people stay in shitty jobs about six months longer than they should. I found myself thinking, *My God, I've been doing this for a year—a year is too long for anything.* The time had come for me to leap into the void again. The administration was removing things from us. Little things at first: complementary copies of exhibition catalogues, coffee in the break room, the water cooler. Soon health benefits started decreasing, and paychecks, never that big to begin with, started shrinking.

The building itself wasn't enough to keep me afloat through the day anymore. I was doing little more than dragging myself home a wreck every night and drinking myself to sleep. During my three days off after every four-day stint, it took me two days to mold myself into some sort of normal human shape and the remaining day to steel myself for the next four. This was no way to live.

After I hit the twelve-month mark, I began hallucinating on post. After six or eight hours on my feet, I'd look across the rotunda and see people transformed into giant tufts of hair slowly shuffling their way up the ramp. Figures in paintings started to move and gesture at me. I stopped understanding my own language. I started drinking on the job, sneaking pulls from the half-pint in my pocket. Most frightening, I got some bad ideas in my head, and started making plans.

Before anything bloody could happen, I split.

LAURA SPENT two or three days a week at a speech research lab in New Haven, so my days alone at home were empty and quiet. I sat on the floor and stared at my feet. I tumbled into a dangerous depression. I switched from wine to whiskey.

Once in a while something would force me to leave the apartment. That was always good. That was why I liked doctors' appointments. With a neurologist following the progress of my brain lesion and trying to keep my seizures under control, an ophthalmologist tracking the deterioration of my eyes, and internists keeping tabs on my kidneys and liver, I had a medical appointment at least once a month.

I always aimed to arrive at the doctor's office an hour, sometimes more, before I was scheduled to see my physician. Not only did it set me free from the apartment, it provided me a whimsical glimpse of some ugly portraits of the human condition. Neurology waiting rooms are much more fun than emergency rooms or psychologists' offices. In shrinks' offices, people keep to themselves, stare at the floor, flip despondently through worthless, outdated magazines. Emergency rooms have all the drama and the blood, the screaming and the gunshot wounds. There's nothing subtle about them—the tragedy is played out on the surface of the flesh. But neurology waiting rooms require detective work. They force you to use your, uh, brain, to decipher the clues to what's gone wrong with the people sitting around you.

Usually these clues consist only of unspoken shakes and twitches, growls, drooling, mumbling. But sometimes there's no guesswork involved. One of the first times I was in the neurology waiting room at New York Hospital, I was sitting across from two tense-looking women. Before long, a crisp young doctor strode in, sat down next to them, and made only the feeblest attempt to keep his voice down.

"Mrs. Marlin, I'm afraid the tumor in your son's brain is completely inoperable. It wouldn't do any good to even try."

One of the women stood up slowly, grabbed two clumps of her hair, and began to wail.

The doctor, who had obviously been playing hooky when they were teaching sensitivity in medical school, tried his best. "Please calm down, Mrs. Marin. There's no need . . . *Please* sit down, Mrs. Marin, your son has a good two or three weeks yet. . . ."

On this visit to the neurologist's, I was an hour and a half early. I sat in the office trying to read Henry Miller and waiting for something funny to happen. Apart from the extroverted— —that is to say, obnoxious—old man to my left trying to convince the Italian woman to my right that he knew Rome better than she did, nobody said much of anything. Then I caught a new voice by the receptionist's desk.

"I . . . I have an *emergency!*" a woman was saying. "I've got to see Dr. McKimmon *right away!*"

This had potential.

The receptionist put in a call to the doctor and told the woman to take a seat. Fortunately, she sat down directly opposite me, which saved me the trouble of craning my neck.

She was older, probably in her fifties, a little overweight. What held my interest was her head, which was misshapen: it looked like a peanut poised atop her shoulders. And her *face*— her face was moving in about forty directions at once. Her eyes were filled with a dark panic, and her mouth spat out grunting, pained sounds. Maybe someone was pulling a *Scanners* trick on her, in which case I should move, before I ended up with her brains in my lap. But the doctor arrived and took her away before her head exploded, so I went back to reading.

Sometime later, the old man piped up again.

"Excuse me, are you a rock star?"

I glanced around to see if one of the Ramones had shown up, only to find that the man was looking at me.

"Pardon?"

"Are you a rock star?"

"I should think not."

"You're not a rock musician?"

"No sir, no. I'm not."

"You sure do look like one."

"I do not."

"Well, if you're not a rock musician, what do you do?"

"I guess I write funny stories."

"You write funny stories?"

The problem wasn't his hearing, his skull was just three times too thick.

"Yeah, though most people, I guess, don't find them terribly funny."

"Don't find them funny? You know that comedy and tragedy are very closely related."

"That's always been a pet theory of mine, too," I said. I tried to go back to my reading. I only wanted to look at people, not interact with them.

"Say, young man. Where are you from?"

Jesus, I hate that question.

"I'm pretty much from all over the place, sir."

"You sound like you're from the country."

"Uh-huh." I made a point of opening my book and staring at

a page, even if I wasn't seeing a damn word of it. My brain was screaming, *Leavemethefuckalone.*

"I'm from Brooklyn. Born and raised there." He pretended I was engaged in a normal human conversation with him.

"Mph."

"I bet you're wondering why I have this strange accent."

It sounded like Brooklish—a combination of your basic Brooklyn and basic British accents.

"Not particularly."

He finally got the hint from me, but he was still hungry for a victim. He hobbled over to the receptionist's desk, where he picked up the day's appointment list.

"Marjorie DeBonet? I know a Marjorie DeBonet. I wonder if it's the same woman."

The receptionist made a noncommittal sound.

"Is that right? Is this name Marjorie DeBonet?"

"Actually, it's pronounced 'de-bo-*nut*,'" the receptionist clarified.

"Are you sure? Are you sure it's not 'de-bo-*nay*'?"

"Yes, I'm sure. It's spelled N-U-T, not N-E-T."

"Maybe somebody just misspelled it."

"It's spelled correctly. She's in here every two weeks."

"I still think it's pronounced 'de-bo-*nay*.' Is she from France?"

"No, she's from the Bahamas, actually."

I couldn't understand how the receptionist was staying so calm. I was at the breaking point, and the man wasn't even talking to me.

"The Bahamas? Well, does she speak French?"

"She speaks six or seven languages."

"Really? Is she about my age?"

"No, she's probably in her thirties."

"Is she a large woman? Big-boned?"

"No . . . she's quite slender, actually."

I couldn't take it anymore. Something in my brain—probably right around that lesion—went all catywhompus.

"Get it through your fucking skull!" I shouted. "It's not the same woman!"

Suddenly everyone in the waiting room was staring at me.

"What?" I glared at them.

They all went back to their business, and the old man kept his mouth shut for almost a full minute before he started with the receptionist again.

"Do the patients here often talk to you about getting old?"

if i can make
it there

SOME GOOD NEWS came through in July, a year after I left
the Guggenheim. A Manhattan weekly, *New York Press*, picked
up "Slackjaw." I had been in contact with the editors at the paper
since I moved to New York, but while they knew the column and
seemed to like it, they didn't want to run it if it was running si-
multaneously in Philadelphia. I wasn't ready to pull "Slackjaw"
out of Philly yet; I owed everything to Derek at the *Welcomat*. I
wasn't going to turn my back on him for a deal I might be able to
cut in New York.

I did an occasional small piece for the *Press*, a music review
here and there, a short bit about a bowling alley on Staten Island,
nothing much. When a new publisher was brought in at the
Welcomat, a man with small, piggy eyes and a dull wit, Derek
knew it was time to leave. With him gone, there was no question:
"Slackjaw" had to leave, too. It was a matter of honor.

New York Press was a twisted, unpredictable, angry, funny alternative paper, filled with rants and first-person accounts of
terrible lives. After nearly six years of appearing weekly in
Philadelphia, "Slackjaw" left for New York, without missing a
week.

Once again I had some income, better than what I was making in Philly, but hardly enough to pay my share of the rent. I had
to do something else.

Then I remembered my eyes.

The idea of becoming a government leech slammed headlong into my personal morality and pride. Nonetheless I considered it, and concluded I should probably meet with a social worker anyway, to see what my options were. My ophthalmologist had reconfirmed that I had retinitis pigmentosa, that there wasn't a thing to do about it, that I was going to be blind before too long, and that I was, in simple physical terms, legally blind now.

While I could still read fine, and still navigate the streets fairly well in bright daylight, I was losing my depth perception, and my field of vision had shrunk so that I had to swing my head from side to side as I walked, to keep an eye out for things in my path. I could see people walking toward me, but even in the best light I would trip over things close to the ground, like curbs or tree roots. Every day it grew more difficult.

Doctors, shrinks, and Laura had been bugging me to look into disability compensation, since I was going blind and didn't seem to be able to make a living in any normal, reasonable human fashion. My uncle Tom had been living on disability checks for upward of thirty years. Of course, he lived in a trailer park in northern Wisconsin. I had always balked at the suggestion, but I didn't know what else to do.

I was sitting in my social worker's waiting room, where I was finally comfortable with the idea. Those minutes I spent waiting were the last minutes I would be.

The social worker appeared to be pleasant enough at first. She was in her mid-forties maybe, with short hair, haggard; she looked older than she sounded on the phone. I was brought into a tiny, barren office and told to take a seat.

"How is everything going?"

"Fine right now."

A shadow of concern crossed her face. "You expect things to change?"

"Things change every day, usually sometime between five and six. Everything crashes then. Everything dies."

That was a stupid move on my part. I was there to talk about my eyes, not my mental state. I didn't know then that this woman spent half her time as a psychotherapist. She was hooked now, and I could do nothing to get her off the line.

She took a brief medical history and asked what medications I was on.

"Well, I take a gram of Tegretol a day for my seizures, five thirty-seven-point-five Effexors for depression, though they don't do jack shit, and fifteen thousand IU's of vitamin A for my eyes, though that doesn't seem to be doing much, either."

"Any other drugs? Say, *cocaine?*"

Jesus Christ. "No."

"So what else do you take?" Evidently she was convinced that I was on something. I was getting annoyed. I came to see her because I was going blind, not because I was a crack addict. Still, I tried to help her out.

"I smoke. Drink three pots of coffee a day. And I drink some."

"How much do you drink?"

I could sense her questions were getting way out of hand, but I gave her a rough daily estimate anyway.

"Has anyone ever told you that's too much?"

"Helluva lot better than it used to be. I haven't thrown up on myself in a few months now. Because of drinking, that is."

"Has anyone ever told you *one* drink is too much?"

I was trapped in a tiny windowless room with a crusader.

"No, no they haven't, ma'am."

"Would you call yourself an alcoholic?"

Whenever I hear that question, I pull out the old Jackie Gleason line: "No, ma'am, I'm a drunk. Alcoholics go to meetings."

"So that's it? Have you ever considered AA?"

"Alcoholics Anonymous is a religious cult."

"You mean they wear hoods and light candles?"

"Yes, yes they do, ma'am."

"Do you want to stop drinking?"

"Most certainly do not, ma'am."

I was trying to be as polite as possible, but I was getting seriously pissed. This was not what I was here for.

"So why did you come to see me?" she asked, long after passing judgment on me, determining that I was just another shiftless addict there to make a quick, easy buck in order to feed my habit.

"I have retinitis pigmentosa. I talked to my ophthalmologist before I called you, and she confirms that I am legally blind. I'm having a helluva time finding work. It's pretty ugly when I go into a job interview, trip over a table, then have to feel my way along a wall to find the chair. Things are usually pretty downhill from that point on. So I'm wondering what kind of services might be available to me."

That bit about the interview wasn't completely accurate, but I was a desperate man in desperate circumstances. A friend of mine who had done some research for me about dealing with social workers warned me not to say outright, "I would like a lot of money, please." I was playing it cool. Blunt, but cool. Or so I thought.

It made no difference. She wasn't interested in blindness. As a psychotherapist, she was interested in suicidal depression; and presumably as a reformed alcoholic, she was interested in drunkenness. She asked about my income, my home life, my brain damage, and then, after flipping through some sheets on her desk, told me the only things I could hope for were welfare, Medicare, and food stamps.

I could feel the nausea rising inside me. *No.* I wouldn't do it, because I couldn't do it. That old Knipfel blood pride reared its head and screamed. There was a big difference between welfare and disability. At least there was to me. I reminded her that I was there because I was supposed to be completely blind in a few years, because I had a monstrous time feeling my way through subway stations, not because I was lonely and depressed and drunk. She advised me to call the Metropolitan Transit Authority about half-price fares for the visually impaired. She then asked me to rate my emotional pain on a scale of one to one hundred.

"I'd say that I'm at about eighty-eight right now."

"Is that why you drink?"

"It's why I could use a drink right now."

"You know, twelve-step programs really do work."

"Sure, if you're a spineless coward who chants well. That's not why I'm here, ma'am." Maybe humiliation was supposed to be part of the game, from step one.

While she was looking for the welfare office phone number, she asked what kind of writing I did.

"Oh," I told her, absently, "I write funny stories about the stupid little adventures I get myself into."

"You'll certainly get some good stories out of the welfare office, then. It's a *nightmare*." She smirked.

I chuckled weakly back at her. "So what about my eyes? What's the story with disability?"

She thought about it. "Well, apart from calling the Transit Authority, there's not much I can suggest, other than public assistance. If you really *are* legally blind as you say, and if you have documentation to prove it, you might want to try occupational therapy, but you'd need Medicare for that."

What, she doesn't believe me? Why would I make up something so stupid? I have a better imagination than that.

"What would I get from them?"

"They could teach you how to cook. . . . I imagine your wife does most of the cooking . . . ?"

I couldn't believe this anymore. Was this some ham-fisted reverse-psychology technique?

"I'm a helluva cook, ma'am. And I can sweep, and I even do the laundry on occasion."

She went on as if I hadn't said a word, back to the drinking, back to the depression, blaming every dilemma I faced on demon wine. In her mind, I had brain damage because I was a drunk, was ousted from grad school because I was a drunk, couldn't hold a job because . . .

"As long as you refuse to admit that you have a problem, there's nothing anyone can do."

"Thank Satan for small favors," I muttered to myself.

"Sometime you might want to think about stopping entirely for six months, just to see what a difference it would make."

"Ma'am, I drank hardly a drop for the first twenty years of my life—and that's why I started."

I gathered my things and left her office. As I pulled my coat on and reached to loosen a smoke from the pack in my pocket, I thought, *Fuck it. Feet or knees. Always the fundamental question. Feet or knees.*

I crumpled the card with the phone numbers she had given me and let it drop to the floor, then headed out to find the nearest bar.

"TURN OVER."

Huh?

"C'mon, turn over, we gotta take some X rays."

Those are the first words I remember. Before that, I was

walking down the street, on my way to meet Laura and a friend for a matinee. Now I was—who the hell knows? I was turning over for whoever wanted me to, and passing out.

It's funny the things you accept when you have no idea what's going on. *I'm wearing a neck brace. Oh, the pillow's soaked in blood.* The past several weeks had been building to something bad. I had been sinking deeper into a more volatile depression and paying for any brief flashes of joy with days and weeks of abject misery. The drinking, which was always a cheap excuse to kill pain, was slipping out of control. And now I'd blown it. Again.

The next time I woke up in the hospital bed, screams and howls on either side of me, I waved my free arm around until a nurse's face was gazing down into mine.

"Yes?"

"Excuse me, but can you tell me what the hell happened?"

"You don't know?" She walked away, and I passed out again, conscious only briefly of the fact that I had a bunch of needles stuck into my left arm and a fierce need to relieve my bladder, but still not knowing how I'd gotten here. Or where, exactly, here was.

A CHINESE DOCTOR was staring down at me when my eyes opened this time. "You were very drunk," he said. "You don't remember what happened?"

"Can't say as I do."

"You were very drunk, you passed out and cracked your head open, then you had a very bad seizure."

Things were slowly coming back to me, in shards and flashes. I had met a friend for lunch. I had ordered the first round. I vaguely remembered leaving the restaurant. Then I was someplace in the East Village, trying to reach the movie theater at

Eleventh and Third. I wasn't exactly sure where I was. Beyond that, I couldn't remember anything.

I waved a nurse over to ask if anyone had called my wife. She walked away without a word. I still had to piss, and eventually persuaded an orderly that I was serious. He brought me a plastic cup.

"What the hell do I do with this?" I asked him.

"Put it between your legs."

I tried to go about this with one arm full of tubes, voices around me wailing, "I need a doctor! God help me, I need a doctor!" and nurses walking past, flapping my robe down and saying, "Oh, you've got to keep that covered up."

Some nine hours after I first blacked out, Laura called Bellevue—the hospital where I didn't know I was—for the third time, after a frantic search for me. She had phoned police precincts, hospitals, the Transit Authority. By this time, around a quarter to eleven, my name had made it into the hospital's computer system.

So while I lay there like the stupid, foolish, hopeless goat that I was, Laura, together with two of our friends, dealt with the Bellevue bureaucracy.

"Did the doctor tell you everything?" one of the nurses asked my wife.

"Well, how would I know if he didn't?" she replied, a University of Chicago graduate to the core. The doctor asked her repeatedly if she was okay, and if I'd ever been to AA.

Laura didn't seem terribly happy to see me, and I can't say as I blame her. At about twelve-thirty, the hospital discharged me, complete with a bill that misspelled my name and listed a wrong address, phone number, birthdate, and Social Security number. My hair was thick with caked blood, the back of my skull felt soft, and my left shoulder was immobile after the tetanus shot I'd been given.

As I pulled on my clothes, I took inventory. I had passed out on the street, had had a seizure and lain there for Lord knows how long, and then I'd been taken to Bellevue. Who knows what had disappeared along the way? Wallet and keys were still there, and three dollars in cash. My silver flying-eyeball pin was still fastened to the lapel of my jacket. Smokes still there. Lighter. First (and only) edition of *The Suicide Cult*, the first of the Jonestown exploitation paperbacks. Directions to the movie theater.

"I don't suppose the EMS folks bothered to grab my hat, did they?" I asked, without much hope.

Laura reached behind me, picked it up from the bed, and slammed it down on my head. As we walked out, I reached into my jacket pocket for one last thing.

"Aww, shit."

"What is it?"

"Someone nabbed my knuckles."

"Well, they probably aren't real comfortable admitting armed patients into the emergency room."

"Yeah, I suppose."

I've been through worse, I've been closer to the big sleep, but somehow this trip shook me up more than the others. I felt I was getting old, and if I wanted to get any older, it was probably time to rethink a few things. The final delight of the day was waiting for me in the mail on the kitchen table when I got home. Some charming, anonymous soul from Philadelphia had sent a postcard inscribed, in very neat red letters, "FUCK YOU—I pray for your death."

The next morning, Laura told me that she refused to live with this kind of behavior anymore, she just couldn't, and if anything like it happened again, she was splitting.

A few weeks later, even though I hadn't passed out on the street or thrown up on myself, Laura packed a bag and moved out. She had had enough of me.

Laura and I had been together in one way or another for four years before we were married, then another four years after. Now it was all over. I put on some Sinatra, poured myself a drink, and lay down on the floor.

"WHAT?" I asked her when, soon after, she stopped by for some of her things.

She shook her head at my question, half smiled bitterly out the window, and muttered, "Nothing."

"Don't give me that. What's wrong?"

Silence.

"You're killing yourself, you know," she said, finally.

"Oh, well."

"Well, so what do you intend to do about it?"

"Work a little bit harder, I guess."

When we had first started seeing each other, when once a month I rode Greyhound the ten hours from Minneapolis to Chicago to see her for two days, wine was an integral part of what held us together. We'd start on the first bottle the moment I got to her place, and then keep going. Those were the good times. We rarely left her matchbox of an apartment, we ordered take-out, kept meaning to watch *The Night Stalker* but then forgot to. All the drinking we did then was happy drinking; it was love in a bottle.

When we moved to Philadelphia, Laura would proudly proclaim herself a lush. While I degenerated into a raging, self-mutilating monster, the result of my as yet undiscovered brain damage, we still took weekends off, stocked up on red, white, and bourbon, never bothered to get dressed, cooked for each other, stayed as far from sober as we could. As long as I could keep my brain under control, as long as we could keep Philly ignored and outside, things were good.

Even in earlier days in Brooklyn, back when I was at the Gugg and we had money to splurge every now and then, the wine held us together. We'd buy a couple of cases of a cheap French white and go through them both in a weekend. When money was low, we would settle for a gallon jug, chill it, then open it and leave it on the kitchen table. Every time we passed by, we'd refill. That was a few hours' worth.

But something changed. I thought, hazily, that Laura was losing her stamina. She used to match me bottle for bottle, smoke for smoke, but she was slowing down. She would complain about getting only a few swallows from a bottle, until she insisted on using two glasses. Then she complained about getting only one glass out of a bottle. Or two bottles.

She asked me to promise that I'd make a fifth of Wild Turkey or brandy last more than two days. At first I figured it was a money thing; we could hardly afford to be dropping as much money a week as we were on alcohol. We'd stopped going to bars, except on special occasions. But over the months, her urgings became more intense, until the night she had to pull me out of Bellevue. That was the end of it for us.

SOME PEOPLE DRINK because it's Christmas Eve and they want to celebrate. Others drink just because it's Christmas Eve. You could say I fell into the latter category.

I'm not sure how this came to be. When I was a kid, I got as

excited about the holidays as any midwestern kid. I set out cookies and milk for Santa; I didn't ask any questions about how, exactly, he was supposed to hit every house in the world. As long as
he hit mine, it was okay. I wallowed in it, filled with a warm and
joyous greed.

Something happened back there, though. Something, somewhere, turned to dust. I remember sitting in the dark in my par-
ent's living room when I was fifteen or sixteen, in a chair next to
the Christmas tree, my nostrils filled with the heady scent of
fresh pine, looking out the window at the lights blinking on the
other houses on the street, feeling absolutely dead inside. I
vowed to ignore the holidays the best I could from then on. I'd
buy presents for people; I wasn't looking to be hated so much as
I was just looking to be left alone.

After Laura left, it became much easier to hide and avoid the
fact that the rest of the population was running around pretending to be filled with the joy of the season. She used to put up a
little tree or decorate the rubber plant, hang some lights, bake a
lot of things that involved cranberries. Christmas Day she'd actually cook a turkey. This all had a frighteningly traditional air
about it.

My first Christmas Eve alone was chilly but not unbearable.
There wasn't much snow on the ground that year. I don't know
what got into my head, there was plenty to drink in the apartment, but I put on my hat and my long black coat and went outside. Though I still had no work besides my column, I'd been able
to collect a few old debts the week before, so there was some
spare green in my pocket. I took a train into Manhattan, got out
in the East Village, and looked for a bar that wasn't being stupid
about the holidays.

I peeked in at Milano's, a long, narrow old-man place on
Houston Street. I'd never been there before. Four men were sit-

ting at the bar, and there were no decorations that I could see, no wreaths, no nothing. I opened the door, stepped into the warmth, and let the door slap shut behind me. When I took a stool at the end of the bar, no one looked up. The men weren't together, but were sitting one or two stools apart, staring down into their glasses, absently peeling the labels from their bottles. All of them were in heavy coats, all of them in hats, all of them at least twice my age. The battered weariness on their faces told me this wasn't the first Christmas Eve they'd passed here. I ordered a shot of Wild Turkey, paid for it, lit a cigarette, and huddled over my glass like the others.

I threw the whiskey back and ordered another. As the evening wore on, I switched to beer. I needed the first couple of whiskeys to kick-start me.

One of my companions went to the jukebox. I was afraid he would put on something like "Blue Christmas" or "Merry Christmas, Baby." If he did, I would have to leave. But a few seconds later, out came Sinatra doing "I'm Not Afraid." I never believed Sinatra as he sang it, and I don't know that I was supposed to. That song brought the first smile to my face I'd felt in months. Dammit, we were all afraid, all five of us sitting there, but we were not about to admit it.

Although we never spoke to one another—nobody said a word except to the bartender—we took turns going to the jukebox and selecting another set of Sinatra, or Tony Bennett, or more Sinatra. And although nobody said anything, each new song was met with silent approval, a finger tapping on a bottle, a head bobbing along to the beat.

The bartender bought us all a round or two without ever saying "Merry Christmas." Now and then the door would open and people would come in, a few groups of two or three, but they never lasted more than one drink. Maybe they left so quickly because they had some party waiting for them, but I preferred to think that they were driven out by the combined psychic force of five old men who didn't want to be bothered on this most joyous of holidays.

Yet in fact there was warmth there, an unspoken camaraderie. We all knew what the game was, and we all knew we had lost it big-time. We'd been shut out, but it didn't matter. We had our beer, our whiskey, our vodka and gin, our smokes. And while the rest of the world was gathering in warm circles of friends and family, exchanging gifts and holiday cheer in a cheap attempt to reach deep into the human spirit, the five of us had found what we needed.

Soon after midnight, more than a little unsteady on my feet, my vision a shaky blur, I slid down from my stool and fumbled to the bathroom. Once inside, I could hear that someone had punched "Cycles" on the jukebox, for probably the sixth time that night. *So I'm down, and so I'm out, but so are many others. . . .* I zipped up, stepped back out into the bar, and leaned on the jukebox until the song wound down. *But I'll keep my head up high, although I'm kinda tired, my gal just up and left last week, Friday I got fired. . . .* Then I buttoned my coat and stumbled out into the horror of Christmas Eve in New York, leaving the four men sitting at the bar. I'd just experienced one of the most touching, honest Christmases I could remember. At the time, of course, I couldn't remember much.

I USED TO SAY, only half jokingly, that I was born with an infant's body and a hundred-year-old's spirit. That I was an old man's soul trapped in a young man's aging body. Yet as my body grew older, my spirit was getting younger. I was living in reverse time. I'd seen this happen in other people. Derek was approaching sixty, but he had the spirit of a twenty-five-year-old. When I took him to see Killdozer, a raucous punk band from Madison, who played in Philly a few times, he put me to shame. He was a wild man, a bearded troll bopping this way and that as I slid toward oblivion at the bar in back.

My gait was increasingly slower and shorter; I was reduced to a hunchback shuffle. This was just a survival technique; if you move slowly and keep your arms close around your ribs, then even if you run into something, as I was prone to do, it won't do as much damage. Soon the survival technique became the only way I was capable of moving, and my arms twisted into a permanent gnarl.

Obvious questions arise when the eyes begin to die: How will I read? How will I write? But other things, the basic, trivial things life is made up of, worry you just as much when darkness creeps in from the corners. Like banking. ATMs are out of the question. At the bank I go to, there's a strip of Braille along the bottom of the touch-screen machines. I don't read Braille and can't say I ever will, but I suspect this strip says something like, "Give it up, jackass, this is a smooth-touch screen. You're shit out of luck."

Then there's my apartment. I learned some time ago that I really do have to follow the common dictum of a place for everything and everything in its place if I'm ever going to find anything. I try to put books, pots, bottles in specific places. No matter how conscientious I am, I can't avoid mayhem. One night, reaching for an aspirin bottle, I misjudged where I was standing and thrust my hand deep into the box where I keep big kitchen knives. I quickly pulled it out, slashed and dripping. Another night I picked up an ashtray from the floor and put it, I thought, in its place next to the television. The next morning I discovered that I'd instead shoved it into the VCR.

I try to keep things off the floor to avoid kicking or stepping on them. I push chairs in under the table and leave doors open. I sweep every weekend or two. Still, the decay closes in. Living with beasts doesn't help. In the middle of the night, I'm awakened by the sound of books crashing to the ground from a high shelf. Fucking cats. In the morning I look for the damage, the spilled books, but I don't find anything until, some days later, I kick them by accident.

No matter how I try to clean the place, I always miss some spots; tabletops, cabinet doors, and corners become thick with impenetrable grime. I find piles of cold cigarette butts on the bathroom floor, days after being sure I've flushed them away. The infinite puddles of cat vomit I find only when I slip on them. I lose things inside refrigerators and cabinets and closets, and forget about them. And yet the apartment could be infested with millions of roaches and armed battalions of Norway rats, and it wouldn't bother me because I wouldn't be able to see them.

We often read or hear news stories about people found living in abject squalor, and the same question is asked: How could they live like that? Maybe like Ruth, my neighbor in Minneapolis, they're just people who are tired and sore, and want nothing more than to be left alone with their memories:

Sixteen, seventeen years old, bowling ball on my lap, squeezed between Mike Butry and Dave Hansen in the backseat of Robbie Reed's ramshackle '72 Buick. Robbie behind the wheel, his slow-witted brother, Tim, in the passenger seat, Ozzy on the stereo, the five of us screaming along that barren stretch of Allouez Avenue, watching the speedometer bounce between 105 and 110, scared to death that Saturday morning, expecting to die, but laughing wildly all the same.

public transportation

"Dr. K, look, we've got an idea." My editor at *New York Press*, John Strausbaugh, was on the phone.

"Yeah?" I had no clue where this was leading.

"You can take it or leave it, but we're just tossing it out there."

"Okay, what?"

"Would you be interested in being the receptionist here?"

"What, at the paper?"

"Well, yes."

I'd done it before. Filled in for a week between the previous receptionist and the present one. On Tuesday of that week, the phone had woken me before my alarm went off. The sun was up, and I rolled out of bed and padded into the kitchen and waited for the machine to answer.

"Jim, you there? This is Sam."

Sam was another editor at the paper, a fellow about my age who'd done much better for himself than I had. I picked up the receiver.

"Hey, Sam," I grumbled, pushing the hair out of my face.

"Dude, where are you?"

What an odd question. "Why? What time is it?"

"About eleven."

"Christ." Goddamn alarm. "I'll be there soon as I can."

I reached the office half an hour later, assumed my post at the front desk, and profusely apologized to everyone who passed by. I finished out the week without further incident. Now I was being offered the same job full-time, so apparently I had recovered from that potentially fatal error. At least nobody was mentioning it. They would later, when they wanted to embarrass me in public or keep me in check.

"Yeah, that sounds fine," I told Mr. Strausbaugh.

"You'll be facing some pretty tough opposition. Some of the folks in the sales department didn't think you were too nice to them last time you did this."

"I didn't know being nice was part of the job."

"It's worse than that, actually," he said. "Some of these people are under the impression that you're some kind of Nazi."

"Where in the hell'd they get that idea?"

"Probably your stories."

Jesus. "I'll be a fuckin' sweetie-pie."

"That's what I like to hear."

Strausbaugh and the other editors were getting tired of stories about how I was starving to death, spending my days all bunched on the floor. It was a cheap and easy way for them to get me out of my apartment, onto the streets, into the subways, where I could find something more interesting to write about than chasing mice around the room. And for me, it would mean a regular salary, something I could live on. Pity job or not, I was happy to take it.

The first thing you learn as a receptionist is the art of lying. In every office, there are people who, through tireless effort, have ascended into positions of power, where they no longer talk to people they don't want to talk to. They can pay desperate and hungry others to deal with the unpleasantries of day-to-day existence for them.

I had a list on my desk of the people to whom the folks in power were willing to speak. If the person who called wasn't on that list, I would put him on hold for a while, then come back and say, "I'm sorry, but Mr. Bryson seems to have left his desk, would you care to leave a message?" And if I thought the message wouldn't merit Mr. Bryson's attention, it was my job to crumple it up and throw it away before he was forced to waste his time reading it (given, of course, that I had bothered to write it down in the first place).

Then there were those dozens of people who called every day to make sure that their faxes had arrived. "Can you just run and see?" they would ask, not realizing, or maybe fully realizing, that the *Press* received hundreds of faxes a day, that the fax machine was a quarter-mile from my desk, or that I was working ten phone lines at once. My first week full-time I tried to explain all this, but the callers got snippy. So I started telling them that, sure, I'd run back and check; I'd put them on hold for a few minutes and then inform them everything was hunky-dory. That way, everybody was happy.

My favorite callers were those who got really, really pissed at me when the person they wanted to talk to wasn't around.

"I've called him five times in the last *hour!*"

"Ma'am, have you considered waiting longer before calling back? Increase your chances that way."

"Can't you go take a look for him?"

"Nope."

"Thanks for all the help, asshole!"

"My pleasure, dimwit."

Lying is an ugly word. The central skill any receptionist worth his or her sweat must master is *misdirection*. Where I worked, I had to deal with more than the recommended daily share of stalkers, psychotics, struggling artists, and panic-stricken foreigners. My duty was to get freaks off the phone or out of the office as quickly as possible, leaving them with no desire to come back. This is where I was transformed into the doorkeeper in

Kafka's "Before the Law." Most everyone I considered a friend was a freak, a psychotic, or a struggling artist. Come to think of it, most were all three. Most of the people I knew were full of horrific tales about how hard it was to get past some cold, snotty, uncaring receptionist to speak with the people in power who might be able to help them in their career. Now *I* had become the one who was blocking their path.

Sometimes the voice on the other end of the phone told me I was dealing with a ragged housewife who doodled pictures of kitties on the side and considered herself an artist. She would insist on talking to the "man in charge" about a job as an illustrator.

"Look, ma'am. Face it, I'm being straight with you. You'll never, ever get through to him."

"Why not?"

"Because he doesn't want to talk to people like you."

"He'll want to talk to *me*."

"I know where I can get twenty-five-to-one odds on that. Ma'am, why don't you just give it up?"

I wasn't usually that blunt. Only when the voice was supremely stupid. As I said, the art of being a successful receptionist is the art of misdirecting, convincingly. You have to make callers or visitors believe that the person they want—no, *need*—to talk to really is in a very important meeting, instead of sitting back at his desk, doing funny tricks with a pencil. If they don't believe you, they'll call or return an hour later and annoy you further.

When I started, I was flabbergasted at the level of stupidity I had to deal with. I spent far too much time one day trying to explain to some bright boy how to dial a phone number when he'd been given only letters to punch. "Well, sir," I advised, "take a close look at the keypad. . . . You see how there are three letters next to almost every number?" Another young man, obviously a struggling genius, became so incensed after not being chosen one of the paper's restaurant critics that he phoned every two or three minutes for six hours, just to call me, the receptionist, who had nothing to do with any hiring decision, ugly names. I guess he needed a job, too.

I tried to write my stories at work—that seemed to be part of the deal, I had a computer at my desk—but soon discovered that it was impossible. The phone never stopped ringing, and a never-ending parade of delivery men came through the door. I had to put off my own work until the weekends.

I had gotten spoiled, being unemployed as long as I had been. I had twenty-four-hour days all to myself to do what I wanted, even if all I wanted to do was smoke, drink, and mope. More important, though, I had been able to live like my new bosses. I dealt only with people I wanted to deal with, except when I was forced into the grocery store or the bank. Of course, my bosses make lots of money doing this.

WHEN MY EYES were stronger, my subway routine went like this: The train doors would open, I would step aboard, make a quick scan to find the most promising freak or lunatic, and then try to get a seat as close as I could. Now, with my field of vision shrunk to the size of a dime, I was satisfied simply to find any seat and sit down.

One night on my way home from work, I nabbed the seat directly to my right when I entered the car, pulled out my book, held it close, and started reading. Over the top of book, on the floor, I saw a pair of bright white, expensive-looking tennis shoes. I paid them no further mind and went back to my book. It wasn't until the doors closed and the train started moving that the man who filled the shoes started talking.

"I'm the craziest!" he shouted. "I'm the crazy-assed!"

That was his line, which he repeated in tones approaching a howl. I didn't look up. I was tired and cranky and wanted to read. Then I heard another voice.

"Hey, man, you better put down that bat." I looked up.

The huge man in the white shoes standing in front of me was balancing a baseball bat over his left shoulder.

"I'm the craziest!" he screamed. "I'm the *crazy-assed!*"

Now I realized I was alone. Everybody else was crowded at the other end of the car, packed side by side, staring warily at the crazy-assed with the bat. My skull was poised beneath his elbow, begging to be a home run.

Oh, Christ, I thought, *I'm in no mood.* Some time ago, I would've egged him on, prayed him to take me out of the game. After a few weeks as a receptionist, dealing with lunatics and fools daily on the telephone and in person, I was bored, annoyed, and experienced. I didn't move to a new seat; I knew I was facing a wild animal and that any show of fear or recognition would make me the obvious target. I sat still, tried to remain invisible, made no sudden motions, and read my book while he kept announcing his condition and jostling the bat on his shoulder. He took no notice of me, and when he got off at a stop in lower Manhattan, the rest of the passengers spread out and took their seats.

On another day, after a bad nine hours at work, I squeezed into a car near the back of the train, wriggled my way down the line of people, found space on a pole, and settled in. I stared out the window at the darkness and the passing lights, listening only to the arrhythmic groan and squeal of the wheels along the tracks. I needed a drink.

All around me, people were muttering—about jobs, kids, union politics. Somewhere amid the hum, I heard a familiar name.

"Green Bay," someone said. "I spent a lot of time in Green Bay, Wisconsin."

Well, I grew up in Green Bay, I thought to myself, in a reflexive, banal way. It wasn't unheard of to come across someone who'd lived there, of course; I'd met a guitar player in New York who had worked in a car wash near the Tropicana go-go bar in Green Bay. Still, it wasn't every day I heard people mention it on the subway.

I looked around, trying to figure out who was talking.

There he was, a kid a full head taller than I, late twenties maybe, with a puffy blue jacket, leather cap, cropped hair, sharp features, and a fresh-scrubbed look about him. An athletic type. Lots of kids in Green Bay looked like that, and many of them had beat me up at one time or another. It wasn't until later, if you stayed in Green Bay long enough, that the strange, lumpy growths appeared.

He was talking to two younger women who were staring up at him in wide-eyed adoration. He was the center of attention, he was gonna get him some, and he was happy about it.

"After Wisconsin," he told them, "I moved to Chicago."

Hey, I moved down to Chicago after leaving Wisconsin, too! I thought in that same banal way.

". . . then to Minneapolis . . ."

And to Minneapolis, too! What a remarkable series of coincidences.

"And then I went to Philly for a few years . . ." The young women cooed at his obvious worldliness. I wondered if this series of coincidences was just a tad too neat.

". . . before I finally moved to Brooklyn a few years ago."

"And is that when you started writing for the paper?" one of the young women asked.

My body went numb—that tingly numbness that hits in an

instant, in moments of revelation or mind-scrambling fear: *This man was pretending to be me.*

"No," he went on, chuckling softly in a way I never would. "I didn't start that until later. Only about two years ago. Before that I worked as a security guard at the Guggenheim."

"That's right." One of the young women turned to her friend. "I remember reading about that."

Pretending to be me? How stupid can this man be? Why doesn't he pretend to be someone from Pearl Jam, or Robert De Niro, or one of the Baldwin brothers, someone worth his while? Who would want to be me, anyway? I don't even want to be me. He doesn't look or talk like me. I would never wear a puffy jacket or a leather cap like that.

Then I stopped myself. *Calm down,* I thought. *You're exhausted, you're cranky. This is some kind of delusion. It's happened before. So he lived in the same places you did, worked in the same place you did, and writes for some kind of paper. It doesn't mean a damn thing.*

This almost worked, it almost got my breathing back to normal, until one of the girls asked him where the name "Slackjaw" came from.

This is no dream! I thought, leaping back to that scene from *Rosemary's Baby.*

"Well"—he chuckled that stupid chuckle of his again—"that's a secret of mine I'd rather not talk about."

"Asshole!" I wanted to scream. "You don't want to talk about it because you don't know the answer!"

Why at that moment I didn't work my way over and say, "You, sir, are an impostor!" I don't know. Maybe I should have, but part of me wanted to see how far he'd take it. Besides, at least this meant somebody was reading my stories.

When I was writing for the *Welcomat,* now and then someone would claim to be me to get into a show or cadge free drinks from a bartender. I even encouraged it, figuring it would mean no one would be sure what I looked like.

But now on the subway a thought too monstrous to consider seriously crept into my head. *What if he is me? What if this is the form immortality takes, and that fool standing ten feet away is my replacement?* I half expected the ghost of Rod Serling to step aboard at the next stop to explain my predicament.

My mind filled with visions of the Fake Me hopping off at my stop and reaching my apartment before I did. I'd check my mail, find nothing, walk upstairs, and open my door, only to see him sitting at the kitchen table with my cat Evil on his lap. She'd give me the kill-eye, and her low growl would rumble from deep in her guts. He'd stare at me and smirk. I kept a close eye on him as the subway barreled ahead.

We pulled into the station before mine, and the Fake Me got off, his groupies in tow. This stop was almost equidistant from my place as my regular stop, but I never used it because the walk home required navigating a block invariably cloaked in darkness. It was where I had had the shit kicked out of me by two young thugs a couple of years earlier. The Fake Me knew that. Being athletic and able to see, he could only have been planning to sprint to my apartment and get comfortable before I got there. And I still had to stop at the store for milk.

By the time I reached my apartment, I was sweating despite the chill air. I opened my mailbox. Nothing. I ascended the steps slowly and silently, listening for the stereo. Lord knows what CD he'd have popped in. Probably jazz. He looked like someone who would pretend to enjoy jazz.

I slid the key in the door. It worked. He hadn't monkeyed with the lock yet. I stuck my head in and looked around. Both cats sat on the floor, yelping at me for having left them alone all day. My stomach settled, and I told myself, *I've really got to do something about this paranoia.*

I WAS RETURNING to work on a downtown number 6 train after another delightful visit to my neurologist's—I was nearly on the nod, as the wacky German nurse had drained what seemed like a gallon of blood from my left arm—and I sat down across from two bums, one black, one white. They were whispering to each other and giggling, and making sinister hand gestures. Then this woman got on. Severe-looking, though she might have once been pretty, acting as if she still were. She sat down next to them, right next to them, even though the car was half empty, and tried to weasel in on their plans. The two bums were surprised, but before long they accepted her and spoke to her as though she'd been there all the while. After several stops she got off, just as abruptly as she'd gotten on and joined them.

Both the bums looked straight ahead toward me. They were still talking to each other, but something about the conversation had changed. Now they just took turns repeating the conductor's announcements.

Conductor: "Twenty-eighth Street."
White bum: "Twenty-eighth Street."
Conductor: "Twenty-third Street."
Black bum: "Twenty-third Street."
And that's all they did until I reached my stop.

This reminded me of a subway ride a few years earlier. I was coming home to Brooklyn after a few miserable days in Philly, and it hadn't been a good afternoon. I was tired, beat, out of money, I had no job, and things weren't going well with Laura.

I got on a downtown A train at Penn Station. It was about six-thirty on a Friday, so things were tight, but I found a seat. Across the aisle from me sat an old woman who appeared to be in worse straits than I was, with a shabby coat and a kerchief knotted loosely around her thinning hair; her face expressed the most abject misery.

She casually reached into her handbag, a little purse held together with packing tape, and pulled out a monster wad of bills. A huge fucking roll of bills, which she proceeded to count. Tens, twenties, fifties. Maybe this was everything she had left in the world, but it was a lot more than I had at the time. It would have been so damn easy: I was armed, and surely I could run faster than she could. I'd never mugged anybody, at least not for money, but I was right there at the end of my line, and I was willing to give it the old college try.

My face must have played my thoughts out loud and clear. I stared hard at the bills as she counted them. I was suspicious — why was she flashing the roll like that on the subway? was she suicidal? was she insane? was she an undercover cop?—but I didn't care, and I had nothing to lose. I could follow her when she got off and make up my mind then.

Suddenly I felt the light touch of fingers on my knee. I looked up, startled, into the grim face of an old-timer next to me. He'd been there, he'd been young and brash once, he knew the game, and he shook his head gravely at me, his eyes sadder than death.

He was right. It would be wrong. I hung my head in shame. I wasn't sure if he was scolding me, though. Maybe he was warning me off a setup. Maybe he was trying to save me. I was considering whether to thank him, when the train stopped again. The Wad Woman got off, my Guardian Bum a half-step behind her. He hadn't been scolding me or warning me off at all. No, he was telling me, "I saw her first."

I'm not sure why this came to mind as I sat on the number 6 watching those two bums scheming, except maybe the fact that both episodes seemed to involve the plans bums make on trains. I was working about a gallon low after the visit to the neurologist's and it'd already been a hell of a day.

In the office that morning before the appointment, seizures kept washing over me. During one of these spasms, I had to arrange for FedEx to pick something up for a bigwig. I shook like an animal as I tried to spell my name for the FedEx operator, who made fun of me.

"K-N-I-P-F . . ."

"Gee, how do you pronounce that again?" she drawled.

I tried to tell her, through clenched teeth. The phone was crushed against my ear, and my hands, balled into fists, were squeezing into my forehead.

"You should pronounce it differently."

I grunted.

"Don't mind me," she chirped, "I'm just goofy in the head today."

Yeah, aren't we all.

Coming to work that morning, I had left behind me in my apartment a dead telephone and a bathtub faucet that kept spitting out scalding water, even though I'd shut the water off the night before. The tub didn't bother me so much—I could pretend I was living next to Niagara Falls. But the phone got to me.

For the past few months, the static on my phone had grown steadily worse. I'd attributed it to sunspots, even though nobody I knew was having similar trouble. This went on until one night something in the phone imploded, and the system went dead. Flat dead: no clicks, no buzzes, no rusty hums, nothing. It wasn't that I was going to miss chatting on the phone; it's just that I was still a touch paranoid, and was convinced something horrible was going to happen to someone I knew and I would miss the funeral because my telephone couldn't handle sunspots.

So as I sat on the number 6 train watching the two bums, I had two thoughts.

First, despite all the shit that rained down on me every day, I really didn't worry about too much. Everything was here and then gone. Pain slammed into me, then it passed. The stupid, ridiculous situations I found myself in didn't mean much, they were simply things that happened. I complained, sure, but I didn't worry. The fact that there was no order, no direction, wasn't bothersome. I can't say I didn't have a care—I simply *didn't* care.

Second, everything that happened, each drop in that same rain of shit, chipped away, weakened the structure. Things come and go, but they always take a little bit with them.

These thoughts stayed with me, pounded me from inside, when I got back to work, then later when I rode home, ate dinner, showered, went to bed, got up the next morning, showered again, dressed, and drank cold coffee. When I sat down to put on my shoes, both cats yelped at me to stay home and play. With their noise and the windows closed, I didn't hear the hubbub outside.

When I stepped out, queasy and unsteady in the morning sun, I walked into a movie shoot on the sidewalk at the bottom of my steps. A big production, with trailers, klieg lights, cameras, cables everywhere, people scrambling about like roaches.

"What in the hell is this?" I shouted at the people blocking my gate. Dozens of bleary and angry eyes turned toward me. I glared back. I had to get to work, and they were in my goddamn way. I stomped down the steps, shoved my gate open, and stepped carefully past the snaking cables, aiming for the free zone a few yards away. I still can't help wondering if, of the twenty-three takes of my stairs done that morning, they'd decided to use the one where the weird guy in the hat walks out his door and yells, "What in the hell is this?"

My day was already in a tailspin. And whatever was behind it—karma, aliens, sunspots—would go into overdrive.

Two blocks from my subway stop, a block before I left the quiet residential street for the commercial district, I saw two people wrestling on the corner before me. It wasn't just any two people: that would not have been so unusual for the neighborhood. These were two female crossing guards, both in uniform, having themselves one mighty catfight.

"You gotta go to the hospital!" the woman on top was screaming.

"The hell I do!" the other screamed back, scratching at her opponent's face.

I was either dreaming, in which case I should just enjoy the show until I woke up, or I was being handed a series of bad omens, in which case I should turn around and go home. If Alexander the Great had headed out with his troops one day to conquer Hibernia and the first thing he ran into was a film crew outside his tent, and then a crossing-guard catfight, doubtless he would have postponed his invasion until at least the next day.

Unfortunately, I'm not as wise as Alexander, and I was expected at the *New York Press* switchboard, so I plodded on toward the subway.

On the platform, a fool with an acoustic guitar was earnestly singing Beatles songs. My befuddlement sank toward nausea. When the train arrived, I sat down and tried to cool the burning in my head. One stop from my destination, the doors opened and people got off and on as usual. But minutes went by, and the doors didn't close. Everyone on the car remained stone-faced and silent. We sat as if pretending not to notice that we were just sitting there. More people got on. The train didn't move.

More minutes passed, and the conductor barked for the brakeman over the P.A.

The doors stayed open, still more people got on. Finally the conductor announced: "Excuse me, ladies and gentleman, but we have a sick passenger in the last car of the train."

That was it. I would get off and walk. The mythical sick passenger on the subway could be suffering from anything from a nosebleed to eight gunshot wounds. I was in no mood to hang around and find out which.

I stood up, negotiated my way through the other hopeless souls, and broke free through the open doors onto the platform. It wouldn't be such a bad walk. Just a few blocks farther than usual, and I was early anyway. I'd have time for a smoke or two. What I needed was a drink. I decided to spend my lunch break at Spring Lounge.

I paid no attention to where I was going and stomped up the stairs. Looked familiar enough. I went through the turnstiles and lit a cigarette as I climbed the steps to street level. With my eyes down I kept walking.

It took me a few blocks to realize I hadn't crossed any of the streets I was supposed to cross if I was headed in the right direction. And it took a few more blocks to realize I was walking into the morning sun. I stopped. I pictured a map of the United States, the sun rising in the east. I zeroed in on New York, then on Houston Street. I was going in the wrong direction.

I changed direction, and a block later a young guy, what some would call a street tough, fell into step with me.

"Brought you white ass into the wrong fuckin' neighborhood, man," he informed me.

"Tell me about it." I kept walking.

He stayed with me, his end of the conversation degenerating into little more than sputtered obscenities.

"Fuckin' . . . fuck . . . fuckin' . . . fuckin' dick . . . shit . . . fuck."

"Tell me about it."

After he saw fit to turn, a man walking toward me caught sight of the big Residents eyeball on my shirt and screamed, tunelessly, "Here I come, Constantinople! Here I come, Con-stan-tinople! I am coming, Constantinople, here I come!" By now, this seemed perfectly normal.

I glanced at my watch: I had fifteen minutes to get to work on time. It was too hot out. I stood next to an elderly Asian man, waiting for the light to change on Houston Street. Just a few more blocks to the safety of the office.

Safety of the office? What kind of madness was I slipping into?

To jar me back to reality, the Asian man started whacking at my left ankle with his cane. At first I thought it was an accident, an old man getting the shakes, so I stepped out of his range. He sidled over to me and whacked me some more. I zipped through the early-morning death race of cars to escape him and lit another smoke at the opposite corner. Maybe I was just hallucinating. It had certainly happened before.

A few minutes later, I opened the office door to find the dear old receptionist's desk waiting for me like a trusted friend. At the stroke of nine the phone rang, and I was soon trapped on the line with a man who insisted on speaking with someone no longer among the living.

"I'm sorry, sir, but she's no longer with us."

"The hell she isn't! Put me through!"

"I'm real sorry, sir—"

"Sorry, my ass! I demand to talk with her this instant!"

What could I do? I hung up and strapped myself in for the day. As if the morning hadn't already made me sapped and grim.

Twenty minutes later, a fellow called to recite some kind of beat poetry:

*"Goat's breath camouflage
Of some peculiar dust of madness
Floating on the smell of rotting chicken
Over America's industrial landscape
Of death."*

There was a long pause as I tried to decide how to respond. I came up with, "Can I transfer you to anyone in particular here in the office?"

"No, no, I just wanted to share that with you."

"Oh . . . uhhh . . . well, thanks, I guess."

"Sure thing!" he chirped happily before hanging up.

Yup, I thought. *Goddamn sunspots.*

Just as I was getting settled into my chair after an unusually tense lunch, everything uneasy in my belly, I got another sunspotted call.

"Are you Mr. Knipfel?" an old woman's voice asked.

"Yeah," I said. I should have known better.

It was a very kindly old lady, who had just gotten around to reading a story I'd written a few weeks earlier about how my cat Evil was infusing my brain with bad spirits while I slept.

"I have cats, too," she said. "And let me tell you, one time, I had the gout? In my foot? And one night when I went to bed, one of my cats slept on that foot, and the gout went away like that."

"Uh-huh." I looked around for someone to share this with, but I was alone.

"And another time? I had serious chest pains, and when I went to bed, another of my cats slept on my chest, and the next morning the pains were gone."

"Well, ma'am, that's very nice." I assumed she was finished. "I'm glad things worked out for you. But here's the difference between us. Y'see, you have good cats. My cats aren't good. Not at all. I have an evil, *wicked* cat who does bad things to me while I sleep."

She wasn't happy to hear this negative attitude. "Well, I'm just calling to say that I think you should continue to let your cat sleep on your hand."

"Oh, I don't have much of a choice in the matter, ma'am. If I don't let her sleep on my hand, she'll hurt me. And bad."

"How could she ever hurt you?" The woman sounded aghast at the notion.

"Oh, ma'am, she's got these sharp claws and teeth—"

I didn't want to be mean to a person who seemed very nice, but the conversation was going on too long and I had other calls to answer.

Goddamn sunspots.

By four that afternoon, I figured I was in the clear. The cretins who had called since the cat lady were typical day-to-day cretins. I knew them all very well. Maybe more shrill than usual. But soon another call reminded me of the recent cosmic events.

"You can stop making crank calls now, asshole," the sharp young woman on the other end spat.

"Excuse me?" This one caught me off guard.

"I said you can stop making crank calls."

"I'm afraid, uhh . . . what?"

"For the last three hours you've been calling me and hanging up whenever I pick up the phone. This last time I hit star six-nine, and this is the number I got."

"Well, ma'am, look, I'm a receptionist. I have neither the time nor the energy nor the inclination to spend three hours making crank calls. There are a lot of people in this office, so if you have any idea who it might be, I'd be more than happy to put you in touch with them." I was curious myself.

She seemed to believe my story, and I was awfully glad. Many callers didn't believe what I told them, and presumed me responsible for most everything that was wrong in their lives and the world.

"I think I know who it might be," she said, finally. "I'm going to hang up now, and if it continues, I'll call you back and tell you what her name is."

Her? Well, now, this was heating up. I was hoping this woman would get one more of these crank calls, even if it was just by accident.

I never heard back from her. And I hadn't asked her for her name or number, under the circumstances.

The next morning, on the train into the city, I thought I had broken the spell. I thought a few beers and a good night's sleep had cleared the effects of the sunspots. I was riding smooth and easy.

At the East Broadway stop, a well-dressed man got on the train, knelt on the floor in front of me, and without saying a word, began methodically to remove his clothes.

f l u b b i t y - f l u b b i t y

AS THE FADING LIGHT in my eyes accelerated toward darkness, the folks around me, parents, friends, various eye doctors, insisted that I get myself either a cane or a dog. I put the kibosh on the dog notion immediately. The cats wouldn't stand for it, I had no room for another animal, and I was too much of a hermit to take a dog out for walks a couple times a day. Since my ophthalmologist maintained that a foul, drooling dog could not be substituted with my choice, a seeing-eye rat, I voted for the cane.

Laura and I had been on friendly terms since she'd left. She had been bugging me more than anybody about the cane. So one Saturday, I let her drag me to the corner of Fifty-ninth and Park in Manhattan, home of the Lighthouse, a foundation established to help the blind in a multitude of ways, and Spectrum, the Lighthouse store. Spectrum was full of neat things for people like me, a Sharper Image for the blind: clocks and telephones with REALLY BIG NUMBERS; talking clocks; clocks that crowed like roosters, in case you wanted to pretend you were living on a farm; magnifying screens for computers and televisions; high-contrast-LED cooking appliances; radios and other mundane appliances with big knobs.

Laura led me around the store, pointing these things out. To me, everything remained pretty much a blur, each display bleeding into the next. There were few definite edges, and fewer discernible independent objects. Only when things were pointed out to me, only when I was given some parameters to work with, would I be able to focus.

In one corner of the store, next to a selection of games for the blind, was a mad supply of canes, all of them red and white. I didn't see any with silver wolf's heads. That's what I wanted.

A fellow came over and asked if we knew what the store was about.

"That's why we're here. Looking for a cane," I told him.

"Who's it for?"

Laura tapped my head to indicate that I was the blind one. I looked at my feet, embarrassed. I was afraid he wouldn't sell one to me. Unless you saw me trying to find something I had dropped, or witnessed me running into something or making a vain attempt to get through a doorway, my condition wasn't immediately obvious: I didn't wear dark glasses, didn't have whitish roving eyes, didn't carry a tin cup full of pencils. But the man didn't seem to doubt me.

It was news to me that the canes came in different sizes, that the optimum length for a blind man's cane was sternum-high.

"That's the length they've figured lets you tap out the distance of one full stride in front of you and two inches to either side of you," the clerk explained. He pulled various canes off the rack and held them up to me. Finding one of the proper length, he asked, "Are you taking classes yet to teach you how to use one?"

"Well, not yet . . ."

"I ask because giving you one of these without the proper training is like handing a set of car keys to someone who's never driven before."

I had a flash of my own fiery death, my body being cut out of the jaws of a twisted, smoldering mass of cane wreckage.

My problem with the training business had started several

months before, when I contacted the Lighthouse about just that. I had come home from an ophthalmologist's appointment with a headful of bad news, and in a panic, I gave them a call. I was told that I could either pay $250 for classes and start right away, or wait for government funding. I chose the latter, not having a spare $250 lying about. I was reassured to know that the well-oiled machinery of government was grinding away already, eager to take care of one of the nation's cripples.

Here it was, months later, I was still waiting for the government to get back to me about cane training.

I bought the cane, and Laura and I left the store and popped into a bar a few blocks away.

"Here's to accepting the inevitable." I raised my glass in a toast.

"No, here's to actually *doing* something about it, asshole," Laura replied. I suppose I hadn't been very cooperative up to now.

I didn't tell anyone, but I was disappointed with the cane. I couldn't very well beat any of my assailants to death with it. It was a collapsible model, pretty much the only kind that's made anymore, four sections held together internally with an elastic band. Sure, I could whack somebody, but it would just go *flubbity-flubbity-flubbity*, and my assailant would say, "Hey, cut that out, you!"

I wanted something deadly. Something oak or cherry with a silver wolf's-head handle. The guy at the Lighthouse store hadn't understood what I was after. If I was looking for a "support cane," as he called it, I'd want to go to a surgical supply store.

No, I thought, I'd want to look in a tobacco shop, the only place where walking sticks with style and class and menace about them are sold anymore. I went home, where I opened a beer and chased the cats around the apartment with my new blind-man stick. One of these nights, they really would suck the breath out of me as I slept.

I COULDN'T SHAKE the notion of a cane with a silver wolf's-head handle. That was what I wanted.

The next morning, I put something on the stereo and went about my morning business. Then it was time to pull myself together, grab a quick beer, zip into midtown, and buy me a nasty walking stick. It would be easy as pie. I knew what I wanted, and where to find it: the Nat Sherman tobacco store in Manhattan. I made it there with no trouble, no bruises or scrapes, no getting lost. Only when I got inside did my troubles begin.

It being a Sunday, the place was crowded. It being small, I was buffeted back and forth among the rabble. It being dim, I was frustrated as all hell. I shuffled a few steps this way (no canes, just cigars), and I shuffled a few steps that way (no canes, just pipes), and I shuffled a few steps over here (no canes, just lighters and fancy ashtrays). I decided to ask someone, but found myself at the end of a long line of asshole cigar-smokers. I had smoked cigars when I was younger, but that was different. These people were animals.

"I'm looking for something . . . opulent," I heard one arrogant prick tell the woman behind the counter.

Finally I found a salesclerk, a pleasant young woman who sent me to inspect a dark case full of walking sticks with dolphin-shaped handles. Dolphins I didn't care about. I wanted wolves. If no wolves, then snakes. Something with some guts to it. She told me there were more canes upstairs.

Taking the small, careful steps I take when I'm not sure of my surroundings or my destination, I eventually got myself to the second floor. I was stopped by a man in a light-gray suit and an Andy Warhol wig.

"Can I help you?" he asked.

"I'm looking for a walking stick."

He sniffed in an imperious way I'd heard described but never witnessed firsthand, and looked aside.

That was rude.

"Am I headed in the right direction?" I asked the back of his head.

He swirled back around. "Well, what are you *looking* for?"

"Walking sticks."

"What?"

"Walking sticks."

"Wakkastys? What? I simply can't under*stand* you."

I bet if I had said, "But I am *French,*" he would have understood me without a problem.

I cleared my throat. "Canes," I said.

Painfully he lifted a finger, pointed to a corner, and heaved a tired sigh. I shuffled away.

My first and most reasonable impulse was to grab the nearest stick and beat his soft head in, beat him straight the fuck into the ground, but I didn't. Even though there weren't any silver wolf-heads in the collection, I knelt and checked prices.

One tag said $125.

Another, $295.

If I wanted a hand-carved ivory bust of Beethoven perched on the top of my new cane, I'd be expected to shell out $600. Not the type of thing I'd want to get all bloody. I realized I'd entered another little world I didn't belong in. It was time I went home.

Unfortunately, I discovered, the nearest subway entrance, at

Forty-second and Sixth, had been closed. Middle of a Sunday afternoon. No cops around, no fire trucks, and no explanation. I started working my way north.

God damn.

The train I hopped on at Forty-seventh was headed in the wrong direction, so I got off at Fifty-third to transfer. As I was walking down the platform, keeping close to the wall the way I always do for fear of slipping and falling onto the tracks, some Transit Authority workers threw open a door. It slammed me hard on the right and nearly knocked me to the tracks anyway. I picked myself up, limped along, and eventually made the transfer. One stop later, a large man in an expensive-looking suit got in the near-empty car and sat down across from me. He had that bad look in his eye. Sure enough, before I'd seen the lights of the next station, he was at the door next to me, pounding the glass with both fists and kicking at the stainless steel with his right foot, muttering sounds that were further from English than anything my cats could muster.

When he got off at Thirty-fourth, I glanced at the woman a few seats away. We gave each other the "Well, what are ya gonna do?" shrug.

After so many days like this, I had to wonder: Was it just me? If someone else experienced all these tiny failures, would he look at them as simply minor annoyances, or would they take on the extravagant mythological proportions that they did for me? Was it a matter of my living in the third person, looking at the whole mess and every mess that made up the thirty-year tragicomedy of my life, or was it indeed strange that these things happened to me? Damned if I knew.

That night, back on the bottle, I talked to Laura. We were complaining about this and that. This time, though, rather than being tugged at by explosive anger, I felt cold as a hangman. In the eight years we spent together, she had learned that I gave up all hope far too easily.

"You aren't going to do anything stupid tonight, are you?"

I thought about it for a second. "Naaah . . . I'm not that far gone yet."

"Promise?"

"Yeah . . . yeah, I promise," I muttered.

I decided to wait a few months instead.

DESPITE A LIFETIME of bitterness, littered with more than a dozen conscious attempts to murder myself, one phrase, one thought, has resurfaced regularly. This is as close to a personal mantra as I will ever get: Deal With It.

This guiding rule has helped me through most of the crises and thousand humiliations that gnaw at me daily. It even worked somewhat with the encroaching blindness.

I had known for a long time that the light in my eyes had been fading since childhood. I even bought that damn cane in acknowledgment that I'd have to deal with my blindness sometime. The light had been fading at such a snail's pace that I could set every minimal decrease in vision aside and say, "Okay, so now this is what you can see, and this is what you *can't*. Deal With It." But one autumn night in 1996, that notion crumbled into ash.

I didn't trip over garbage cans or run into a wall, I wasn't assaulted by scalawags, and I didn't crack my skull open again on a sidewalk or a pole. No, in fact, I made it home physically unscathed. But that night, a fundamental realization surfaced: Some things simply aren't worth Dealing With.

On the way home from work, I stopped to check in on Grendel, Laura's cat. She was going to be out of town for a few

days, so I told her I would stop by and feed him. I got to the apartment at quarter after six. Fed the cat. Sat down and lit a smoke
while Grendel munched hungrily away. I cast a wary eye toward
the window. The sky was getting dark too fast, and I didn't know
the neighborhood well enough. I felt I was in an old werewolf
movie. I grabbed my bag, pulled my hat on, and fled for the train
through the blue-gray dusk.

Dusk has always been the worst time of day for me; there are
no shadows left to work with, and the streetlights haven't come
on to illuminate the sidewalk yet. I made it to the train, went a
few stops down the line, and headed for the stairs, which would
lead me to whatever daylight was left.

There wasn't much. On the sidewalk I was forced to stop
every few yards, whenever I knew I was approaching people, so
I didn't run headlong into them. I went into the grocery store for
more beer, and by the time I came out, the darkness was complete. I couldn't see a thing. I heard voices around me, voices and
footsteps and the scraping of baby carriage wheels. I didn't dare
move in any direction, for fear of planting a foot in the middle of
some fool's child.

That's it, I thought to myself, *I can't live this way anymore.
This has gone beyond the bounds of the deal-withable.*

It was a slow and agonizing stretch of sidewalk, an entire
block's worth, to my apartment. With each step I hoped my foot
didn't get wrapped in a tree root, a kid, a front gate, or a garbage
can. My wide-brimmed hat, in theory at least, was supposed to
give me a split second of warning, like a cat's whiskers, before I
slammed my head into a lamppost or a wall. It might help me
avoid another concussion.

Once I found my building, it took another ten minutes to get
inside. I stood on the top step fumbling through my keys, trying
to see in the glint of the streetlight which was the copper-colored

one for the front door. There were no lights on in the entrance, so I felt around for the mailboxes, then for the lock on mine, then for the mailbox key. I used both hands to maneuver the key into the hole. Got the mail. Now the vestibule door: find the key, find the lock. Once I had gone through that, things were easier, if only because, having lived there for so long, I knew to avoid the bike on my left and the radiator on my right. I knew where to reach for the banister, and I knew, approximately, where the stairs began. After that, I was home free.

Once upstairs and in my apartment, hopeless, deranged, I felt my way to the kitchen table, groped for the lamp, and almost started laughing when the bulb blew. I turned on the overhead light and waited for the glorious fluorescence to stream into my eyes. I reached above the sink, pulled down the whiskey, and poured myself a shot.

Except for the job, why did I even bother going outside anymore? Christ, plenty of grocery stores in the neighborhood deliver. What more did I need?

Deal With It.

People asked me what I was going to do when my eyes went completely, and my answer was always the same: "What the hell do you think? I'm gonna pump a bullet through my brain."

Even before my eyesight really dimmed, I'd never been that stable. What else was there to do now? What else could I do, except maybe become a poster boy for some blind retard foundation? Fold paper cups? Sell pencils? Thank Satan for computers, since the light source from inside the machine blasts straight into my eyes. I'll be able to work until the last minute.

I had become increasingly chained to my apartment. I had never much liked going out before, even when I could see, but now, whenever someone asked me to stop by, or meet at a bar, or go out to dinner, my throat tightened, dread filled my guts. "I'll see what I can do," I'd say. It wasn't good. The fear of getting lost, of ending up injured, and worse, of being helpless and looking like the fool I was, prevented me from doing the rare thing I occasionally wanted to do. I was too goddamn proud.

When you're going blind, you're suddenly at the mercy of the sighted.

When darkness envelops me, I shut down. If I'm in a bar or a restaurant and I can't see, I don't talk much. Sometimes I don't talk at all; I sit and stare at the blackness. I don't understand why, but then, I don't understand why I'm so obsessive about brushing my teeth, either.

I hid out at home. The world I lived in grew smaller and smaller, the bare walls closed in tight, the cats annoyed me. Things were slipping out of control again. It wouldn't be long before I started wearing Kleenex boxes on my feet and making my few guests don surgical masks before entering the apartment.

A number of organizations in the city tried to help what I loosely referred to as "people like me"—the Lighthouse was one—but there was always something too touchy-feely about them. I would rather go blind and stick a .38 in my mouth than take part in a group hug.

Until now I had been able to avoid such places by Dealing With It in my own way. I would tell people when I met them that I couldn't see and would need to be led around. I apologized to the strangers I kicked, occasionally giving the nutshell lecture about retinitis pigmentosa: "My retinas are dissolving like so many Alka-Seltzer in my head, and right now there's not a goddamn thing anybody can do about it."

I devised my own strategies for survival: reading shadows to determine where steps or curbs began, using my ears as much as my eyes, other phenomenological tricks. But that was all they were, in the end: tricks. Sleights of hand that ultimately did not help.

One of these days, my doctors kept telling me, and I kept telling myself, I would have to learn to use that damn cane. I didn't want to be bitter about it, even if that was my genetic imperative, and in fact I hadn't been that bitter about it. Until that autumn night, my retinitis pigmentosa had been just another physical malady to joke about.

A bigger dread, a silly existentialist hogwash, had crept up on me. I had been frozen to the sidewalk outside that grocery store, unable to move. I was scared. I was almost ready to Deal With It. But not quite yet.

dealing with it

RETINITIS PIGMENTOSA is not as deadly as AIDS, or as painful as cancer, or as crippling as a stroke. It doesn't hurt at all. It only leaves you blind. I will still be able to walk and talk; I won't have to be hospitalized for it unless I run into another lamppost or a moving bus. But it is insidious, and it is frightening.

Statistics show that most people who have RP don't notice the effects until they reach their fifties or sixties. In my case, it started speeding along its preordained course earlier than usual. First the night blindness, then the deterioration of peripheral vision, then the loss of central vision. Most people with RP lose their sight completely by the time they're around seventy. By that time, hell, what's left to see anymore, anyway?

At thirty-two, I had passed through the first two stages, and my ophthalmologist had registered me with the State of New York as legally blind. My central vision seemed to be holding, though; it had always kept me going. Even my central vision had always been far from perfect—nearsightedness and astigmatism in both eyes—but with contacts, I could see clearly enough to read, type, tell what people looked like.

Now, though, in order to read, I had to have a very bright source of direct light over the page, and I needed to use a magnifying glass. In order to identify faces, I needed to move in close and squint. Walking down the street was a matter of guesswork and prior knowledge.

At thirty-two, I entered that final stage. There were no transplants available yet (early human experimentation into retinal transplants had been an unmitigated failure), no treatments, no technologies that would stop the slow shutdown of light. I was unable to read for more than ten or fifteen minutes at a time before the words slipped into a mobile gray blur.

After this began, I stopped going to my ophthalmologist—not the wisest choice. My doctor was among the best in the city, I had heard from several different sources, and I knew the office staff was smart and funny. In the end, however, all they could do was shrug and shake their heads sadly. The only help they could give me, really, was to advise me how to obtain government checks.

In the face of the inevitable, I decided to give away my library. It had always been a source of great pride to me, so this was something I had to consider carefully. And it was something I had to get out of the way, no matter how painful it was.

Over the years my library had been a reference tool for the few folks I would call my friends. They would ask me a question, and even if I did not have the answer handy, I knew it could be found someplace on the shelves, and I usually knew where to find it. Looking for the date Bruno Hauptmann was executed? I have that. Want to know how different translators have handled Nietzsche's nastier side? Here, let me show you. If I couldn't see, if I couldn't read, I couldn't do that anymore. Those books would only mock me. The first editions, the autographed volumes, none of them could represent anything but a deep sadness to me anymore.

I was clearing out not just the books, but a lot of other things as well, for another reason. Even though the apartment was small, narrow, and virtually impossible to get lost in (though Lord knows I'd done it on a few drunken nights), there were too many things getting in the way. Every morning I got up battered from

running into or kicking or cutting myself on things the night before. Misplaced chairs, piles of books and musical records, telephone books (which I hadn't been able to read for some time),
parts of lamps, boxes I was storing for friends. Knickknacks.
Goddamn knickknacks. These were the first thing to go, but I
wasn't always successful. I tried for several months to get rid of a
mechanical severed hand, for instance. A friend from Philly had
given me this life-size, battery-operated, well, severed hand. Flip
the switch and it crawled around. Not much real use for such a
thing, however much fun. But every time I threw it away, it reap-
peared. I'm not sure I want to understand how.

I took inventory, and established that there was a very limited
number of things that I used. One knife. One bowl. Everything
else was in the way. I needed to know where the necessities
were—they each had a specific place where I could find them.
If they were moved, I was lost. And that was another problem
with the library: As the number of books grew, it was increasingly
difficult for me to find a specific one. I knew it was better to end
the frustration, regardless of the regret. Regret I could get over;
frustration was an everyday matter.

AROUND THIS TIME I got a call from Pissbucket, an old
friend from Philly, a writer who had been in a series of punk
bands I had liked. He was busy working two jobs, to support two
children from a previous marriage and his current wife and their
two-year-old. In three months, he told me, another child was due.

Like most everyone, the first question he asked was, "How're
the eyes doing?"

I told him, as I was telling everyone else: "I'm getting geared
up for blind man school." Sometime.

"So what are you gonna do?"

I gave him the spiel about cane training, and Braille, and apartment survival.

"Fine. But what are you gonna do?" Like my ex-wife, Pissbucket had known me too long. He knew the plan. I had discussed it with him too many times. The end of my eyesight meant the end of my life, last he'd heard.

"Whaddya mean?" I asked, all innocent-like.

"I mean, what're you gonna do?" he repeated. I was getting irritated. It sounded as if he was, too.

"Christ, I don't know. Not the slightest idea. I'll make it up as I go along. Just like everything else."

"Not good enough."

"Figured that."

Turns out a lot of other people figured that, too.

A few days after one of my stories in *New York Press* mentioned in passing that I wasn't seeing my ophthalmologist anymore, I got home from work to find a letter waiting for me from Genghis (these folks I know, and all their goofy names!). Genghis was my ophthalmologist's assistant, and a biker. He wrote a monthly column for a glossy biker magazine.

I was expecting the worst—a chastising, a finger-waggle scolding, maybe even threats, from an outlaw, but instead he was friendly and let me know the office staff would give me any support they could. Until, of course, science caught up with us. The next day I got a call from my ophthalmologist herself.

"I'm not calling to tell you that you have to come back," she said. "Genghis was very concerned, and I wanted you to know we're doing what we can for you."

That was swell, but that wasn't all.

"After he told me what you'd said in your story, I made some calls about your case to the State Commission for the Blind, and they got very excited."

"Uh-huh?"

"It turns out you're perfect for them."

"How is that? I've never been perfect for anybody before."

"You're young."

No one has ever called me that before, either, I thought.

"And you're holding down a steady job and you're a writer."

"And I'm blind, too."

That collection of attributes had me in the running to be a social services supermodel. I could see it: Above a photo of me staring blankly at the nothing I could see off camera, the words "Please Give," and beneath the picture, "Jim Could Really Use a Drink Right About Now." If all went well, it wouldn't be long before they had me doing shoe store openings.

What it really meant was that after I finished my basic Blind Man Training, the Man would step in and generously purchase for me the latest high-tech gizmos and whatsits: talking computers, reading machines, the works.

THE DAY BEFORE I launched official Blind Man Training, a fellow at work asked me what my trainers would do to me.

"First thing, I imagine," I told him, "is they're going to give me a tin cup full of pencils and station me on the corner of Forty-seventh and Fifth, just to see how much money I can make."

"Then you know what they're gonna do?" he said. "They're gonna take your hat away and hide it somewhere on the block. And they're gonna say, 'Okay, blind guy, here's your cane. Now find your hat!' "

Another friend of mine had an even better pencil-vending idea. "You know what you do? You take one of those pencils, see, and jab it into people's eyes when they stop, and say, 'Ha! Now *you* can go sell pencils, too!' "

It's good some people can have a sense of humor about my troubles. When the low-vision specialist I would be dealing with called to set up my initial appointment, the first thing she asked was, "So, what have you been up to?"

"Answering phones, going blind. Well, going blind, mostly," I told her.

Her voice turned sad and serious. "I'm sorry," she stammered. She went on to stammer "I'm sorry" to everything I said after that in response to her questions about my deteriorating vision.

Sure, I occasionally get maudlin and self-pitying about going blind, when I start to think about all the things I'll miss seeing. Not trees, though. Everybody says trees. Trees I'm not that fond of. No, there are other things I'll miss: my cat Big Guy's face when I get home at night and he's rocking back and forth on the kitchen chair, frantic to be scritched; the microscopic details of Joe Coleman's paintings; Orson Welles's movies; all those books; the Manhattan skyline at seven in the morning, as the F train pokes aboveground for a stop or two; the glow from the end of my cigarette in a dark bar.

I keep returning to that simple mantra of mine, Deal With It, while recognizing that life has become one long slapstick routine—like living a Marx Brothers movie, except without quite so many musical numbers.

In the doctor's office, I spent most of my time filling out forms. I had been registered with the New York State Department of Social Services Commission for the Blind and Visually Handicapped and had received my official Blind Man Number. I was still waiting for the membership card and decoder ring.

I was going to be taught, among other things, how to use my cane properly and how to read Braille, so I could catch up on the collected works of Tom Clancy, Sidney Sheldon, and Ken Follett. Time to get down to brass tacks.

In one section of one form, I was asked to check off the services I would be interested in. There were basic choices, things I had expected, like mobility training, but there were many I hadn't expected: job-skill training, help in finding a job, help in keeping a job. I checked that last item off. My mind filled with happy visions of Mobsters for the Blind stopping by the office to meet and greet the Men in Charge.

After I completed the forms, I underwent a few hours of tests: field, distance, the same tests I'd been taking since I was three. The reaction I got this time was different.

"You're doing great!" the doctor told me.

Just two weeks earlier, in that very same office, when I'd taken the very same tests, another doctor shook his head and repeated, "Oh, my . . . oh, my . . ."

"Most people your age have lost everything!" this doctor said, too excited. "Most of them are completely blind!"

That, I knew, was a lie. I knew for a fact that most people my age could see perfectly well.

After her happy news, we discussed my training. Three people would call me soon—one for cane training, another for home mobility, another to help me keep my job. Until these three called me, my task was to Deal With It.

"I can do that," I told her.

She pulled out a few gewgaws, one to help me fill out checks and the other to help me isolate lines of text. This would be useful, as long as I happened to be reading mass-market paperbacks.

"Do these come any bigger?" I asked. "You know, for hardcovers or newspapers?"

"No," the doctor replied, "but you can always make your own. There's a paper store not too far from here."

Already I saw it. The subtle reference to my arts-and-crafts skills. I was being softened up to work in a Blind Man Sweatshop where my colleagues and I would fold paper cups or wrap cellophane around slices of American cheese for sixteen hours a day in a Chinatown warehouse.

We talked about schedules and costs, and the doctor placed various low-tech doodads in front of my eyes, to see what they would do. Not much, it seemed. But I guess that was okay, given that I was "doing great." *Jesus.*

The doctor and I shook hands, and I went home to wait for the phone calls. As the sun began to sink, I opened a beer, lay on my bed, and thought about things. I didn't much feel like talking to anyone.

I DIDN'T GET THE CALLS until a few weeks later at work. Hardly before the introductions were out of the way, the questions were flying at me. Of course I wasn't prepared to answer them, not with a dozen phone lines ringing at once and packages coming in and going out. I managed to arrange a meeting with one caseworker.

The morning of our meeting, I stepped out my front door and found a woman and a little girl on the sidewalk at the bottom of my front steps. The girl's eyes grew wide, and she pointed up at me.

"Look, Mommy. Jinx!"

It never ends.

I first had to see my ophthalmologist, and even though my eyes had been dilated, I decided walking to the Commission's office would be easier than taking the subway. Everything was blurry; all I had to do was avoid the blurs that moved.

The Commission's building address was scrawled in fat black

marker on my pack of cigarettes. It was 270 Broadway that I was looking for. I crossed to the east side of Broadway, the even-numbered side, and headed south.

In the 400s someone tapped me on the shoulder as I was waiting to cross the street. A haggard, blurry young man.

"Do you know where the Social Security office is?" he asked, nicely enough. I guess I looked like someone who might know.

"No, I'm afraid I have no idea."

"You got no idea."

"Nope. Nosir. No idea at all."

"I hate you," he said softly, leaning toward me, pleasantry gone.

"That's all right," I replied. "I hate you, too."

"Then we're all set!" he barked with a smile. He stuck out his hand and I shook it. The light changed and we continued our respective searches.

As the building numbers dwindled, I felt more relieved. I have a terrible time finding a place I've never been to on my own before. Once I have found it, I never forget where it is, but finding it to begin with is a nightmare. Now it seemed it would be easy enough, and I had plenty of time to spare.

I read the numbers: 346 . . . 292 . . . 280 . . . Then a sneaker store, and on the next block a park. But the buildings across from the park had already jumped to the 260s.

God damn.

Around and around I went, up one block, then down another, in a futile search for a building that apparently didn't exist. Was this just another cruel joke to play on a blind man?

I bought a can of soda and lit a smoke, then sat at a concrete chess table in the park to weigh my options. After a while I decided I had no choice but to ask. I hate asking for help. But more and more often now, I was forced to. At the next table, a down-

and-outer was rearranging things in his ballooning collection of plastic bags.

"Excuse me?" I inquired without getting too close. I didn't want to startle him. "Do you know where Two-seventy Broadway is?"

Without a word he raised a finger and pointed across the street.

As it happens, 270 Broadway is the anomaly, an even-numbered building on the west side of the street.

Once I got through the front doors, I was in near-total darkness. This is a nasty tendency I've discovered in places that are designed to "help" the blind. Wills Eye Hospital in Philadelphia was the worst in this respect. The reception area is a cavernous, unlit room scattered with floor-to-ceiling concrete pillars. You could sit there all day and be entertained by the zany antics of blind people walking headlong into post after post, like a giant pinball machine. Here at 270 Broadway, at least, there was only a long unlit hallway.

I asked a man where the elevators were, and he said, "Right over there," which, of course, helped me not at all. Once I did feel my way to the elevators, I found a man down on his hands and knees inside, banging away with a hammer at a piece of metal that had come loose.

Things improved when I found my caseworker's office.

"What we're going to do to push this through faster than it would go otherwise," she told me, "is claim that you need all this training immediately in order to hold on to your job. We'll call it an emergency."

"That sounds fine."

"See, if you have a job, it's important to the Commission that you be able to hold on to it."

"That sounds fine, too."

Unfortunately, the fact that I had a job and a regular income, no matter how paltry, meant that I wasn't eligible for the high-tech gizmos I was hoping for.

"We'll take care of your training, that won't cost you a thing. But you'll have to talk your boss into buying any special equipment you might need."

"Uh-huh. I guess then I'll just do without."

I went home to wait for more phone calls.

MR. VERA AND I exchanged messages for well over a week before we hooked up. He had been designated by the Commission to be my Home Survival Trainer. That wasn't exactly what the Commission called him, but that's the way I'd been thinking of him. We agreed he would stop by my apartment at eleven one Saturday morning.

When my door buzzer sounded at eleven on the dot, I felt my way downstairs without the slightest idea what to expect. The voice on the phone had sounded East Indian. When I opened the door, there stood a tiny, round man, Peruvian, I would learn, a full head shorter than I was. I'm not sure what he was expecting, but I probably wasn't it, either.

I led the way upstairs, opened my apartment door, and nudged one of the cats out of the way. Mr. Vera dropped his coat on the bench, pulled a pile of paperwork out of his bag, set the pile on the kitchen table, took a chair across from me, and got down to business, ignoring, or pretending to ignore, the big sign over the table: "Kill or Be Killed."

"Do you cook?" he asked.

Having been forced to talk to people as a receptionist over the past few years, I often found it hard to give simple answers to simple questions. "Well, I tell ya," I told Mr. Vera, "there was a time many years ago when, I must say, I was quite the cook. Why, I could take a . . ."

Mr. Vera waited patiently before asking more pointedly, "What about now?"

"Oh. Now, well, now I just mostly take things out of the freezer and pop them in the oven for twenty minutes."

We got into a tiff over the microwave. I'd never liked the microwave, ever since my dad warned me about "all the evil microbials those things send dancing through your food." Mr. Vera thought I should use it, to remove the immediate threat of burning myself horribly. I stuck to my guns. Some of the worst burns I'd gotten came from trying to remove things from a microwave.

"Mm-hmmm." He made a note on his legal pad. "What about cleaning? Do you have trouble cleaning?"

We looked around the kitchen, at the smoke-stained walls, the grimy stovetop, the crunchy floor. It used to be white, my floor.

"Some," I said, hoping the Commission would spring for maid service.

"Mm-hmmm."

After asking a few similar questions, Mr. Vera outlined what he would be teaching me every Saturday afternoon for the next few months. Then he pulled a catalogue from his bag and flipped through the pages, stopping now and then to furiously jot a note on his pad, and informing me as he went along: "Now. I'm going to get you *this* and *this* and *this* and *this*. . . ."

I listened in wonder to this stranger at my table, who was telling me about the fabulous presents he was going to get me. And like most presents, these were things I would never buy for myself—a talking clock, a watch with big numbers, a large-print address book, oven mitts that went way up the arms.

I wondered whether he could get me a whole suit like that.

Kind of like an attack-dog trainer. But I never voiced my thought. This was serious business.

Mr. Vera went on telling me about the things he would be ordering for me. Some of them were downright silly.

"Now, when you are pouring liquids into a glass," he said in a clipped, lilting voice that still sounded East Indian to me, "how do you keep from pouring too much and overflowing?"

"Usually I just stick my finger in there. When my fingertip gets wet, I stop pouring."

"Very good. That's what we would train you to do. But I had a man once, who asked, 'What about when my fiancée is over? I can't stick my finger into her glass.'"

I raised an eyebrow but said nothing.

"He had a point," Mr. Vera continued. "What about company? It would be rude."

I interrupted him. "Well, for one, I don't get much company. And when I do, uhh, most of them actually expect me to stick my finger in their drink."

"I'll tell you what I'm going to get you anyway. It's a stick that you put in a glass, and when the liquid reaches the top of the glass, the stick begins to whistle."

"That's very odd."

"It's better than spilling."

I backed off.

Once he'd listed all the presents he was going to get me, he warned me that it was very important that I whittle things in the apartment down to the bare minimum. I explained that I was in the process of doing that, giving the library away and tossing out boxes of files and important records every week, transforming a cozy, warm, slightly cluttered homestead into a cold, stark bunker, ready at all times for outside attack.

Then I thought about the contradiction we had here: I was

supposed to be paring myself down to the bare minimum necessary for survival, yet at the same time he was weighing me down
with talking clocks and whistling drink gags.

Before he left, Mr. Vera told me: "Now, if you can think of
anything else you would like, you must let me know in the next
three days. Because if I turn in one list to the Commission, you
will get everything you ask for, but if I have to turn in a second
list, they will be angry, and you will get nothing." He packed up
his paperwork and catalogue and said good-bye.

Later that day, I called my friends Ken and Laura to tell them
about that morning's guest. When I started doing my Mr. Vera
impression, Ken stopped me.

"Whoa now, hold on there a second, Mr. Knipfel. I thought
you said this guy was Hispanic."

"He is. Peruvian, actually, but he speaks with an Indian accent."

"Sounds fishy already if you ask me. Sounds like another one
of them *Knipfel* stories."

I grunted and continued with my tale. When I got to the part
about the two lists of presents, Ken put the pieces of the puzzle
together.

"It seems to me," he said, "like you got yourself a genie."

"Pardon?"

"This tiny, round man who looks Hispanic but speaks with a
weird Indian-type accent appears on your doorstep and offers
you fabulous treasures, says he'll grant you one big wish, but if
you ask for anything after that, it all disappears? Yessir, that's a
genie all right."

Ken had seen through the murky clouds of reason, directly
into the strange heart of the matter.

the cane lady

I DIDN'T NOTICE THE CROWDS, or the trucks, or the smoke, or the fire, for that matter, until I was trapped in the middle of them all.

A sunny day had turned dark on me. It wasn't night, but the sun was gone and around me was darkness, gray and . . . mobile.

The sidewalk in front of me was blocked by firemen and hoses. The way home was blocked by crowds. I couldn't cross the street for the fire trucks, and I couldn't duck into any of the buildings near me because, well, they were aflame.

One fireman in the street called to another, "We should call the chief on this one. I don't know what the hell to do." A Korean woman, sobbing uncontrollably, stumbled out of the smoke toward me and past me into the street, where she kept moving.

I didn't have time to stand around and watch the show. The Cane Lady was supposed to be coming in an hour to teach me, I hoped, how not to wander blindly into fires.

I made my way through the growing crowd, caught sight of light, and headed to Sixth Avenue, over a few blocks, then up to Seventh and home.

AFTER DEALING WITH THESE Blind Man Training folks for not that many weeks, I was already frustrated. I needed the training, and I needed it now. With my working hours, the weekends were the only time left for me to do much of slackjaw

anything—buy my groceries, pay my bills, write my weekly stories for the *Press,* talk to friends, sleep. Weekends were also the
only time I could get the training. But the trainers weren't sticking to a damn schedule. If they had, things would have been so
much easier.

One week, my Home Survival genie told me that he would
be over at nine; he showed up at twelve-thirty. My other trainer,
the Cane Lady, canceled one week for some reason, then the next
week called at eight to cancel on account of the rain, after I had
been up since dawn, running around like a fool trying to get er-
rands done before she showed up. She told me she would try
again the next morning.

At least the Home Survival genie usually showed up when he
said he would. The lesson one Saturday was how to sew buttons
onto tattered shirts with special Blind Man needles.

As we sat at my kitchen table, with me sewing away like a
blind Betsy Ross, he said, "May I ask you a personal question?
You don't have to answer if you don't want to or if it makes you
uncomfortable."

"Every question's a personal question," I told him. "It don't
bother me none."

"Well . . . your marriage. Did your wife leave because of your
blindness?"

I wasn't expecting that. What an odd question.

"Can't say that had much of anything to do with it."

"I was just wondering. Because I often find it the case that
when a man goes blind, his wife starts feeling that he becomes
helpless and too much of a burden."

"Oh. No. Can't say that that was it. Pretty much everything
else was, though."

"Good."

I continued sewing and he chatted away happily about the progress his other students were making.

THE MORNING OF THE FIRE, the Cane Lady phoned to let me know she was on her way. An hour after she said she'd be at my front door, I opened a beer, figuring it was just another prank.

Maybe she was dead or had blown a tire on the Brooklyn–Queens Expressway. She couldn't be lost. On the phone I'd asked her if she needed directions. No, she told me, she knew the neighborhood.

I hit the button on the talking clock: One p.m. Empty day or not, I would rather not spend it at my kitchen table waiting for something that was not going to happen. I'd much rather spend it at my kitchen table knowing that nothing was supposed to happen.

Then I heard the door buzzer.

"I'm ready to scream," were the first words out of her mouth. This was our first meeting, which she had already postponed twice.

"Hello," I said, "come on in."

She was another tiny, round person, with a shock of white bangs, puffy eyes, and a wide, thin-lipped mouth. She looked like an academic. Once her horror stories of road construction were out of the way, she started with the usual questions: family history of RP, personal history with RP, general medical history, medications I was taking, what I could and couldn't see.

"How do you get home from work every night?"

She knew my schedule, and knew that it was dark when I headed home.

"A friend of mine leads me to the train in Manhattan," I told her. "And on this end, well, I've been living in this apartment for about seven years now, I've been walking the same path damn near every day since I moved in here. I guess you could say that I know every crack in these dirty sidewalks of Brooklyn."

"What about curbs?"

She was all right. I had had my doubts from speaking to her on the phone. She had sounded stretched to the limit, no time for another client, but sigh, she guessed she would take one on.

While we talked, a phone that had been dead silent for the morning came to life. As usual, I let the machine answer, and as usual, there was a crazy person on the other end. "Hey, Jim! Y'in there? *Missster* Knipfel? Hey! Wooo-hooo! Hah-*looooo*? Knipfel! Hey!" This went on for too long, yet I sat patiently, occasionally glancing my apologies to the Cane Lady.

"That was my lawyer," I explained when the caller finally gave up. Minutes later, the phone rang again. It was Murray, someone I knew from the paper, calling from Lord knows where.

"Hey, Jim, d'ya hear? El Duce from the Mentors is *dead fuckin' meat*."

I looked down at my hands as he spun out a mercifully brief conspiracy theory about Duce, Courtney Love, and the death of Kurt Cobain. When he had finished, the Cane Lady said, "That sounds interesting."

"I'm just hoping none of the militiamen call while you're here," I replied sheepishly.

She turned back to our business. "You're going to be living in two different worlds, and it's going to be hard. You'll only be using the cane when you need it, but when you pull it out, everything changes. People treat you differently. They figure that you can't see anything at all. You'll find people grabbing on to you and dragging you along, because, of course, they know where you're going better than you do. What I'm saying is that you should be ready for a lot of really weird things to start happening around you."

I thought about that one for a second. "Let's just say I'm used to that."

We went downstairs and outside. The sun was shining. All the doctors and trainers I'd seen for the past several months asked me if the glare on sunny days was a problem for me. "No," I always told them. "Fact is, I need as much sun as I can get. That's why I'd never wear sunglasses." The glare was never a problem, because I always wore my hat and the brim blocked most of the direct rays. Only in the last few weeks had I discovered that without the hat, the sun would drill though my skull like an awl.

We strolled to one corner, and the Cane Lady asked how well I could see the curb, and how far down the sidewalk I could see. Then we turned and went to the other end of the block, where she asked me the same thing. There was no cane involved yet. That would come later. I wanted to ask her if we could go to Seventh Avenue to survey the fire damage, but I didn't get a chance. We went back to my kitchen table instead, where she summarized what we'd be doing over the next nine weeks.

Then she went home, promising to be back at nine the next Saturday. I opened another beer and cleared the messages off my answering machine.

"HOW WILL YOU PREPARE for this photographer?" my genie asked me. We were chopping vegetables for the beef stew he was teaching me how to make. "Will you be all dressed up in your finest clothes?" Being a genie, he spoke that way.

I had been informed by forces more powerful than myself that I had to have my picture taken. I had also been told that there was no escaping it.

I took a big, dull knife to an onion. "Nah, I'll probably just stay the way I am," I told him.

"I think that's good." My genie was extremely enthusiastic about everything. "Let the people see you as you really are."

"Yup, kind of a slob."

This had been a strange Saturday. I had gotten up at six so I could go to the twenty-four-hour grocery before the Cane Lady showed up at nine. The first thing she did when she arrived was resume telling me about a client of hers who had died a week earlier. She had first told me the news on the phone the previous Thursday. What I wondered but didn't ask was, Was this client hit crossing the street or falling on the subway tracks? And if so, hey, just how good a trainer are you? The client had died of natural causes, though exactly what natural causes would take a medical examiner to determine.

In the middle of her story, the Cane Lady reassured me: "But she's not gone yet. She hasn't passed over."

Oh, dear.

"I was talking to her mother the other night, and she told me that she went into her daughter's room, and it was freezing cold. Even the bedspread is freezing cold."

Oh, dear.

"She wasn't ready to go yet. That's where ghosts come from, you know. People who die before they're ready."

"Uh-huh." I had some tapping to do, and her story made me want to get on with it.

Before we went outside with the cane for the first time, the Cane Lady told me about something else.

"There's a program that's going to be starting up again soon," she said, "and I want you to be a part of it."

Whenever I hear the word "program," I think "encounter group." Still, I let her talk.

"It's called the Track Safety Program, the Transit Authority runs it. There's a blind man in charge of the whole thing, and he is just amazing. What they do is they take a bunch of you to the Transit Museum. Have you been there?"

"Sure."

"Okay, they shut down the power—it's still an operating station—and put you in these white jumpsuits, and take you down on the tracks."

This was more like it: "Encounter group faces death."

"They show you where you can stand or lie down so that the train will pass right by you. Or right over you, if you happen to fall onto the tracks."

The program was a few years old, the direct result of an incident in 1993 when a blind woman fell on the tracks and was ground up under the hot steel. The woman had had a guide dog with her, which survived. The dog didn't even end up on the tracks. And people wondered why I didn't want a dog?

The Cane Lady and I went out and tapped around for a few blocks.

I BECAME MORE COMFORTABLE with the red-and-white cane, and had to admit that it helped. Before I used the cane, when I walked home from the subway at night my eyes would strain to absorb the least drop of light available. They would dart back and forth, up and down, for signs of anything I might run into. As a result, I tripped and fell a lot. But with the cane scratching out the sidewalk a step in front of me, my eyes relaxed. Actually, they more than relaxed. They stopped working completely and took a backseat. Available light no longer mattered. With the cane, the only thing that mattered were the vibrations coming through the handle. My eyes had slid into the palm of my hand. Keeping my eyes open, forcing them to do what work they could while I was tapping, only complicated matters.

Several weeks into my lessons, the Cane Lady was trying to teach me the basics of subway travel with a cane. It wasn't going too well.

"It's the furthest one over," the man in the token booth said.

"That means nothing to me," I yelled through the bulletproof glass. "The furthest one over *where?*"

"Over *there.*"

Jesus. I raised my right arm. "Over here?" I dropped it and raised my left. "Or over here?"

This was tougher than I had figured. If you're blind, part of every subway trip involves determining where the cripple entrance in each station is located. I was fast coming to the conclusion that I was going to stick with tokens in the future and not worry about any of this cripple nonsense. Special entrances, special transfer slips. If each trip demanded that I stop at the token booth, I wasn't interested.

The Cane Lady and I returned to my apartment, where she proceeded to play me a tape she'd made of a radio interview with a blind judge who had been nominated for a federal seat. The judge certainly sounded noble.

"So, what do you think of that?" she asked when the interview was over.

"I'm thirty-two years old and I answer telephones for a living. I'm not a judge. I'll never be a judge."

"He was one of my clients ten years ago."

"Really."

"He was impossible to deal with then, but look at him now. He seems to have done all right for himself."

"And how, huh?"

A few hours after the Cane Lady left, my Home Survival

genie rang the buzzer. Why he used regular doors and didn't just appear out of a puff of green smoke was a mystery. Probably too flashy for him. I went downstairs to let him in.

"Hello, Mr. Knipfel! How are you today? How was your week?"

"Oh, fine, fine." I was exhausted from the subway cane shenanigans. "How're you doing yourself, and how was your week?"

"Oh yes, fine. Fine!"

"Well, I'm certainly glad to hear that."

We entered the apartment, and he set straight to work.

"Are you ready to cook a delicious casserole?" he said. "Let's start cooking!"

I followed him into the kitchen, where he unpacked his various groceries. I already knew how to do most everything he was teaching me, and had known for a long time. The problem was, I was usually too tired and drunk when I got home at the end of the day to take the time to concoct a beef stew or whip up a soufflé. It was more feasible to throw a frozen pizza in the oven and crack a beer. I told him this again and again, but he wouldn't have any of it. "That's not Home Survival!" he would say.

I was hoping he would come over every Saturday afternoon to make me a dinner that would last most of the week, but I knew the Commission wouldn't pay for it. When I told my friend Ken, he was incredulous: "Just like you, isn't it? Anybody else would've asked the genie for seventy million dollars. What do you ask for? A casserole." "But it was a really *good* casserole," I told him.

So Mr. Vera and I got the casserole together and into the oven, and as it baked, he asked me if there were any specific problems I was having, Home Survival–wise, that he might help me with.

"I do seem to drop things a lot, knock a lot of things off of tables. Knives especially. I drop a lot of knives."

"You know, most people I have found who drop a lot of things—do you know why they drop a lot of things?"

"They're clumsy oafs?"

"No. They drop things because they are anxious. They are full of anxiety."

"Huh."

"Do you think you are full of anxiety?"

"To be perfectly honest, Mr. Vera, despite everything, despite all the daily traumas, I really don't worry about all that much. Bad things happen, then they go away. I don't dwell on them. Just wait for the next one."

"So it's not anxiety?"

"Can't say as it is."

"There's another reason people drop a lot of things."

"Wait. Before you go any further, can I offer my own suggestion?"

"But of course."

"I think I drop a lot of things because I don't see very well. I run into a lot of things—tables, chairs—while I'm carrying other things, and I drop the things I'm carrying as a result. Does that make sense?"

"Ahhh, you see? Now we are getting somewhere!"

It was as if I was dealing with a shrink. A nice shrink, mind you, a very nice one, and one who happened to be a genie, but a shrink nonetheless.

After he told me the proper way to feel around the floor for things after I'd dropped them, I asked Mr. Vera what was left on his agenda, what else he was scheduled to teach me. He pulled a sheet of paper out of a manila envelope and read down the list.

"Well, let's see . . . I taught you how to identify shirts and pants?"

"Uh-huh. Use safety pins."

"And socks? How to match socks?"

"Uh-huh. More safety pins."

"I taught you how to identify different coins and paper bills?"

"Yup."

"And clean the floor and tabletops?"

I nodded, and he continued, as I grunted an affirmative to each item he read. When he reached the end of the list, he looked up and said, "Oh, I guess we're done."

That caught me by surprise. It seemed to catch him by surprise, too. I thought it was going to be a ten- or twelve-week ordeal, my weekends chopped in half, Saturdays thrown away, but this was only my genie's fifth week and we were already done.

"You mean that's it? That's all I need to know to survive in this apartment?"

That was my genie's cue to give me the official Blind Man Pep Talk, as I believe it's known in the business. He took off his reading glasses, set the paper down, and leaned back in his chair.

"Have you heard of this judge—?"

"Blind fellow, plays golf, was just nominated to be a federal judge. Heard all about him." I decided not to say "noble cripple."

"Yes. And did you know that he was one of my students?"

"No, no, can't say as I did. He was a student of my Cane Lady's, too." I was starting to think that every Blind Man Trainer in New York City was claiming the judge as a former student.

"Let me tell you a story about him. He came to me one day and said, 'Mr. Vera, I have such a hard time when I go to restaurants and order a piece of meat with a bone in it.' He would end up pushing the rest of his food off the plate while trying to cut this piece of meat. It was embarrassing for him."

"Why didn't he order something else? A nice salad, maybe."

"This is just my point. I told him this: When you order a steak, you ask the waiter if he could remove the bone, then cut the meat into pieces for you. And he said, 'Ohhh, Mr. Vera, I could never do that. That is too embarrassing.' So you know what I did?"

"No idea."

"I invited him to lunch with two other blind people, at a place where he'd have to order meat. And when the waiter came, the other two people asked to have the bone removed and the meat cut up into pieces . . ."

This is getting to be a really long story.

". . . and when the waiter came to the judge, he did the same thing. Well, we talked so, and laughed, we had a very nice time. A week later I saw him, and I asked him if he was really embarrassed to order his meat that way. And you know what?"

"No."

"He didn't even remember doing it!"

"That's really something. And now he might be a federal judge."

"The point is this."

Oh, here we go. I can do anything I want to do, even though I'm blind.

"You cannot let the fact that you're blind hold you back from doing anything. Anything at all. If there's something you want to do, but don't know how you can do it, just stop and think about it for a minute, and the logical answer will come to you. Say you want a nice steak, but you don't know how to cook it."

Then I call one of my chef friends and have him come over to cook it for me, have him take out the bone and cut the meat into tiny pieces.

"You think, Should I broil it or bake it or fry it? Well, what you do is this."

Call one of my chef friends . . .

"You try it one way, and if you fail . . ."

Miserably.

". . . you try it another way!"

"That could get awful expensive, don't you think? Especially dealing with steak."

"Yes, but you experiment until you get it right. You can do anything you want to do, if you just stop and think about it."

The pep talk went on for some time, my genie telling me that there would be days when I would be very depressed because I was blind, yet I shouldn't let that hold me back. I tried to explain to him that I was depressed most days, and that it had little to do with blindness. If anything, going blind was giving me a boost. It's a fascinating thing, experiencing the complete collapse of one of your major sensory organ systems. No, I was depressed most of the time because, with the exception of a few brief joyous flutters, my life was a minor train wreck. But Mr. Vera wasn't buying this, either. I dropped things because I was filled with anxiety, and I was depressed much of the time because I was blind. Well, fine, then.

"You're living in a whole new world now. Everything is different, and you will be seeing it all with your fingers."

But the Cane Lady told me I would be seeing everything with my ears, not to use my fingers so much, they'd get cut up and broken.

"In a way, it can be a very exciting experience."

Before he left, Mr. Vera told me he would come one more

week, to make me one last meal, tie things up a bit, give me another pep talk, maybe show me what to do in case of the big fire that would break out while I was trying to fry that damn steak.

THE CANE LADY called me at work on a Friday to confirm our appointment for nine the next morning. She mentioned in passing that since we had had ten sessions together and I had run out of vouchers, she would call my caseworker at the Commission for more. I was confused.

Nobody had ever mentioned that I was on a voucher system. What's more, yes, I was told before we started that I would have ten sessions with the Cane Lady, but this would be only her fifth visit. Something was screwy. As soon as she arrived on Saturday, I brought these things up.

"The vouchers are an ancient system," she said. "Mostly the Commission gives us a set amount of money each month, and we work with that. But they're still using vouchers for you."

I wasn't sure how to take that. "Still, I thought I was supposed to see you ten times."

"And you have."

I thought for a second. First Mr. Vera, now the Cane Lady. Even the trainers were doing what they could to screw over the blind.

"No . . . no you haven't. You have only been here five times. I've kept count."

"Oh no, you've misunderstood. You see, a session is fifty minutes long . . ."

Like a shrink.

". . . and working that way, you've gotten ten sessions. But don't worry. I called and got some more."

Today's lesson, as she'd told me the previous week, would be about shopping at the grocery store. Even though I always made sure to buy my groceries in the early hours, this time I was supposed to leave one thing unpurchased, in order to justify the trip around the corner and up a block.

"So," she said, setting down her pen, "you still need something from the store?"

"That's what you told me to do."

"Good. What do you need?"

"Need beer. I'm running low."

"I like beer, too," she said.

Before we left, she illustrated the proper way to let myself be led around by another person. Most of it was simple common sense.

"Do you let people lead you around now?"

"Sure. Have to."

"Where?"

"Bars and restaurants. Streets after dark. The back area of the office. Stairwells. I'd have someone lead me around here if there was somebody around."

She led me around the apartment, showed me how to get through doorways, that sort of thing. Then she showed me something useful.

"Say you're walking down the street, and someone decides to help you, whether you want help or not. Whether or not you've asked, this person's going to help you. This will happen to you at some point. There are people like that in the world. Whether they're drunk or stoned or whatever, they decide that this is their mission for the day. So someone comes up behind you and grabs your arm without you expecting it. What do you do?"

"Whack 'em with the cane?"

"No, you don't do that."

" 'Cause it'll just go *flubbity-flubbity*?"

"No. You don't hit people. Here's what you do." She demonstrated a very quick, very easy two-part self-defense technique to remove an undesired guiding hand from my arm.

"That's how you let the person know you don't need help. It's all in the element of surprise."

"The element of surprise, yes. *Then* I whack them with the cane, right?"

TWENTY MINUTES after she left, my genie showed up for the last time.

"Are you ready to cook a delicious spaghetti dinner?" He was jovial as always.

"You bet I am!" I had come to feel obligated to adopt an Eisenhower-era enthusiasm when he was around.

"Would you like to cut up this onion?" He held the onion up for me to see before setting it down on the cutting board.

"Get a knife and let me at it!"

As I chopped things up and rolled ground beef into meatballs, I asked him, "Say, when did you learn to make spaghetti this way?"

"Just this morning."

I had forgotten that his first student on Saturdays was a sixteen-year-old blind diabetic in Bay Ridge who lived with his huge, extremely Italian-American family.

"They have taught me many things about cooking," Mr. Vera said, smiling. "And you know, many of the best things I have learned about homemaking I have learned from my students."

I felt a twinge of shame. I hadn't taught my genie a thing. I just took and took and took, squeezing Home Survival tips out of him, then brushing many of them off with, "I've been doing that for a long time now."

We mixed the sauce and set it to simmering, then sat at the kitchen table. He would be leaving for the last time in about fifteen minutes.

"You know," he said, "I am sometimes hesitant to ask questions of my students that might be of too personal a nature." He had prefaced a question to me this way at least once a week since he had started coming over.

"*Pffft*. Don't worry about that. Ask away." And that's how I had answered him at least once a week since he had started coming over.

"Do you think you will ever get married again?"

Again he'd caught me off guard. He'd sort of asked that question already, weeks earlier. Next he would give me the old "If you do, tell her not to move anything out of its appointed place" speech again.

"I can't really say, there, Mr. Vera."

"I tell you why I ask. Because, if you find a girl you like, and you go out with her, and you invite her over to your apartment . . . you might want to get your walls painted."

"Pardon?" He had mentioned the walls earlier, but I had disregarded it. I couldn't see them, they didn't bother me, and getting them painted would be the tremendous pain in the ass it is for anyone, only worse.

"You might want to get your walls painted, and I'll tell you why. Because a lot of people who get involved with blind people worry. They worry that the blind man just wants a maid, someone to keep his place clean. But if you get your walls painted, and she comes over, she will see that you are self-sufficient, that you can take care of yourself quite well, and aren't looking for a maid."

I let this sink in. Was it just his way of telling me I was a hopeless slob?

"That's a very interesting notion, Mr. Vera. Thank you. I'll certainly keep that in mind."

He beamed. Then he stood up, put on his coat, shook my hand, and left. I think he was relieved to have one fewer student to deal with. Maybe that's why he did his ten lessons in six weeks, too. Maybe he was pissed that I had nothing to teach him, only a bunch of stupid stories to tell. I stood at the door and listened to him walk down the stairs.

Not long after he was gone, the spaghetti sauce was finished simmering. I shut off the burner and let the sauce sit. That night I boiled up a big mess of spaghetti, poured the sauce over the top, sat down in front of the news on television, and ate my meal. Half an hour later, I was sick as a dog. My genie had had his final revenge.

encounter group
faces death

I T W A S Q U A R T E R T O N I N E on a Monday morning, and I
was standing at the entrance to the Transit Museum in downtown
Brooklyn. I had been told to be there at nine, that someone
would be there to help me and my fellow Track Safety students
around, that we'd be getting started at nine-fifteen sharp. I was
there early because I always show up early, and also because I
had spent most of the previous Saturday with the Cane Lady
working out the trip.

The instructions I had been sent by the blind man who ran
the Metropolitan Transit Authority's Track Safety Program were
abysmal: "The exit should leave you on Jay St., near Fulton St.
Proceed to Livingston St. Cross Livingston St. Make a right turn.
Proceed to Boerum Place. . . ." For a blind man, or in this case,
for a group of folks who have trouble reading street signs, the instructions were worthless. I talked the Cane Lady into walking
me through the trip that Saturday so I would know where to go
when the time came. Others in my group weren't so lucky.

I stood waiting at the top of the stairs that led down to the
museum; the entrance was blocked by a chain draped at knee
height. I looked up and saw a man with a cane tapping down
Boerum Place. He missed the turn that would deliver him safely
to the museum, and instead headed across the street, into the
path of oncoming traffic. I ran and nabbed him before there was
any carnage, and led him to where I had been standing.

"Those goddamned instructions," he grumbled. "I had to get

here from Staten Island. That means a bus, a ferry, *and* a train. And once I got off the train, Christ, it was go to this street, then find that street. I'm gonna have to have a talk with this character. He's been spending too much time getting driven around in his limousine, if you ask me." The man told me he had finished his cane training a few weeks before.

"A bang-up job they did, too." I gestured toward the passing traffic, forgetting that he would never see it.

He said he worked at a laundromat in Staten Island that was run by another blind man and his blind wife. "I learned more from him about what is available to me than I ever got from the Commission," he said. "All's they do is teach you a few quick job skills and set you loose. They don't want to do nothing else, like Braille. Braille takes too much time for them. They think it's frivolous. They just want to give you these job skills so's you can get out there and support yourself and not bother them no more. So I'm teaching myself Braille now. Correspondence course from this place in Illinois. You should check it out."

"Maybe."

"Hey, are you getting into that vendor's program?"

"I have no idea what that is."

"It's this program the guy at the laundromat told me about. I start in a few months. They put you in charge of these coin-operated vending machines. You take care of them, you make the money. After a while they move you up to these newsstand-type deals, you know, like in the federal buildings. You sell the news-papers and the candy bars, all sortsa candy and shit. You're not getting into that?"

"Well, no. I . . ." I was almost embarrassed to tell him that I had a job and hoped to keep it. But who knows? Things don't work out, one of these days maybe I could be a Snack Man.

As the clock ticked on, I finally asked the question I was most curious about.

"Tell me, how did you lose your eyes? Glaucoma? RP? Diabetes, what?" By all evidence—the cane, the heavy wraparound shades, the wandering into traffic—he was completely blind. That is a rarity. Most blind folks can still see some, at least a little.

It's a dirty little secret most members of the blind community don't want the sighted to know about. Only a very small percentage of the people we call "blind" are completely blind; that is, very few live in complete darkness. Those who do are blind mostly as a result of accidents —like this case in front of me—or birth defects. The rest, myself included, can still discern shadows and movement, light and dark, occasionally even color if it's bright enough, though granted, we can't see these things very well.

"Well," he sighed, as if he had told the story too many times. "Back in nineteen seventy-eight I was mugged by this kid with a broken bottle. He cut open my right eye. Cops never caught him. I had a bunch of operations done on me. Pain like you couldn't believe. Pain I can still remember. Didn't do nothin', these operations. My eye just kept filling up with blood, no matter how many times they drained it. The doctors told me that the left eye would start to get stronger. It'd take over as much as it could. Get more peripheral vision, that sort of thing. And it worked. I could function pretty much normal."

I nodded uselessly.

"Then five years ago, I was doing some construction work, see? And I was opening this thing up with a box cutter, and the box cutter slipped and went straight into my left eye."

"Wow, pisser."

"The doctor said I was lucky that the blade wasn't longer, otherwise it would've gone into my brain and killed me."

I thought, *Sure, if you want to call that lucky*.

At last some people from the museum appeared. They led us downstairs and through turnstiles to a lecture hall in the rear, which stank of vomit, though nobody mentioned it.

There were only four of us in the blind group: me, the guy from Staten Island, an older woman who didn't want to be there, and a college student with a thick Jamaican accent, dreads, and a big, smelly guide dog. The blind man who ran the program, Levy, was short and stocky, very well dressed, maybe in his late thirties. He sat at the front of the room with the supervisor of the Metropolitan Transit Authority's Employee Safety Program.

We had gathered that warm day to learn what, exactly, we should do, if our canes and dogs failed us and we fell from the subway platform onto the track bed below.

The supervisor gave a brief outline of how the typical track bed is laid out: two rails for the trains to ride on, and the deadly, electrified third rail. Then he shared a few anecdotes about people who had fallen onto the tracks and survived.

Next, some practical advice, should we fall: "The first thing you do," the supervisor said, "is scream. And scream loudly. And keep screaming."

Made sense to me.

He and Levy handed out whistles to make it easier.

"Chances are there will be policemen or MTA workers on the platform with you, and they will pull you up."

I wondered when was the last time any of these MTA folks had actually ridden the subway.

"Let a policeman or an MTA worker help you if you can. Only let a civilian help you if neither of the first two are available.

Civilians don't always know what they're doing. If no policemen or MTA workers are available, you might want to ask another civilian to run and tell the person in the token booth that a blind person has fallen on the tracks. The token booth person can't contact the operators of any oncoming trains, but they can call the police, who would then call the MTA's central command station, which would then be able to contact the train operators and tell them to stop."

I raised my hand.

"How long, exactly, does it take for an oncoming train to stop, distance-wise?" I asked.

"If the train is entering the station at twenty miles an hour, figure about two hundred feet. That's with the emergency brake. If it's traveling faster than that, we can't say. There's no set mathematical formula for this, not with so many factors involved. If the tracks are wet, it will take longer. If it's an uphill grade, maybe not so long. Downhill grade, a little longer. For a train moving at thirty miles an hour or more, figure anywhere from three hundred to five hundred feet. Or maybe longer."

"And how fast are the trains usually moving when they enter a station?"

"That depends, too. Whether they're coming around a corner, that sort of thing. There are some stations where the trains come in, jeez, fifty or sixty miles an hour."

What you are saying, I thought, *is that we don't have a chance in hell to stop it before it rolls over us.*

"Second question, is this training offered to regular, sighted New Yorkers? I mean, why isn't it just part of the regular training packet the City hands out to everyone who moves here?"

"No, we don't offer it to the public," Mr. Levy snapped. "And that's because most New Yorkers can see perfectly well. They can see where the third rail is, they can see where the platform is. They can see where to lie down if they have to. They can figure it out for themselves." He seemed annoyed that I was questioning the exclusivity of his baby.

Word came through that power on the tracks we would be exploring had been shut off, and the four of us were handed white plastic coveralls and snazzy "NYCTA" work gloves. We had entered *The Andromeda Strain*, officials leading us single file into the clean, ratless depths of the Transit Museum.

Lesson number one: Never, ever think you will survive by crawling into that cozy space beneath the platform. Nearly everyone I described my training to said the same thing: "I'd just crawl into that cozy space beneath the platform." When the train is bearing down at forty-five miles an hour and you are snuggled under the platform, you are going to be killed, simple as that. And not just killed, but shattered, dismembered, and electrocuted all at once. Because most trains these days have what you call brake shoes, big hunks of electrified steel that jut out from the sides of the train and project underneath the platform, crushing anything in their path. I don't know what else brake shoes are supposed to do, except kill people hiding under the platform.

Lesson number two: If you are on the tracks and a train is approaching and you have the time to spare, walk away from the train.

Lesson number three: If all options fail and you are in an underground station, you can probably lie down in the trough between the tracks and let the train pass over you. A pregnant woman survived that way some months back, we were told; of course, we weren't told how pregnant she was. Most underground stations have concrete beds, with a drainage ditch between the rails. Most aboveground stations have gravel beds, which lack the ditch. Lie down between the tracks there, and you'll just look foolish in your final moments.

I tapped and felt my way around the tracks for a few minutes, asking the guide morbid questions disguised as constructive curiosity.

"How many people fall on the tracks every year?"

"Not too many, really. Maybe half a dozen or so. That doesn't count the jumpers. Them we get more of—you know, suicides, folks purposely jumping in front of the train."

One thing I'd noticed, riding the trains as much as I had: The day after someone died on the subway tracks, the station in question was overwhelmed with the stench of undiluted Pine-Sol and grave mold. Maybe that was simply what subway death smelled like. I wanted to ask the guide about it, but I stopped myself.

Instead, I felt my way to the dead third rail and grabbed hold. Nothing.

"Most of the folks who fall by accident get pulled out, no trouble," the guide reassured me.

"That's good, huh?"

I had long been fascinated by the subway system, and I was thrilled to have the chance to crawl around on the tracks. But I was growing bored surrounded by blind people. These were the first blind people I had dealt with at any length, and all they could talk about, it seemed, were "blindness issues." Blind this and blind that. What blind man is running his own business. Who got a new dog and how it's working out. How the Commission for the Blind was screwing them out of what they were entitled to. And so on. No funny or horrifying tales to tell. Just another tight subculture. After an hour or so, I wanted nothing more to do with them.

Who knew, though? After a few years of no visual stimulation, maybe blindness issues would be the only things I'd be able to talk about, too. I fled the museum, folded my cane into my bag, and went to answer a few hundred phone calls at work.

OVER THE COURSE of the next several weeks, I received a scattered batch of calls from both the Commission and the Lighthouse. I had made the mistake of telling them they would be able to reach me only at work. Which was true, since I left for work at seven in the morning and usually got home at eight or nine at night.

My official Blind Man Training had ended with the Subway Survival event, so I was on my own now, except for these phone calls, which I could neither avoid nor escape.

"Mr. Knipfel?" a chipper voice asked. "This is Marcy, from the Lighthouse."

"Yeah?"

I remembered her and a man from the Lighthouse who had come to the office one day to see how they could make my job easier. I showed them the computer I worked on, the phone switchboard I used, the postage meter in the back. The man told me he had some Blind Man Software he could give me; he would call me the next day about it. The only other thing they suggested was that I get myself one of those closed-circuit TV jobbies.

I had played around with one before. It was a big old box with a camera inside. You slid a book or a paper in on a tray, and the text was blown up on a screen. The trouble was that it cost a few thousand dollars more than I could afford. A woman at the Commission had already told me that at my salary, piddly as it was, I made too much money for the Commission to pay for anything like that. So much for my dreams of being a poster boy.

I hadn't heard from the Lighthouse pair since that visit; it had been four months. Now this perky young woman on the phone

was asking me why I hadn't gotten myself a closed-circuit television yet.

"I can't afford one, Marcy. I answer phones for a living."

"But you didn't even come up to the Lighthouse to look at different models?"

"No, I didn't."

"Why not?"

"Look, you're supposed to be helping me hold on to this job
as long as I can, right? But at the same time, you're asking me to
leave work to go look at these machines, or go to subway training, or go see one of your doctors. All this time you're asking me
to take off work would jeopardize my job a helluva lot more than
the fact that I can't see what the hell I'm doing while I'm here."

"Still, you are sitting there at work every day, suffering." The
sincere plaintiveness in her voice made me respect her just a little bit less.

"I'm not suffering any more here than I do at home. It's just
the way of things."

"But it doesn't have to be. I'm going to call your caseworker
at the Commission and see what we can do for you."

At last count, I had four or five caseworkers. A couple of them
I'd spoken with only once, and that was so they could tell me that
they were my one true caseworker and that I shouldn't pay attention to anything any of the others said. My experiences with
the Cane Lady and the Commission suggested that the various
Blind Man organizations in the city hated one another with a pas-
sion and tried to undercut one another whenever they could, regardless of how that might affect the people they were supposed
to be helping.

"Fine. Knock yourself out," I told her. I had no idea what was
going on, or supposedly going on, on my behalf. All I knew was
that I had phones to answer.

"I'll get right back to you, then," she said, and hung up.

About a week passed and I heard nothing from Marcy. I did hear from one of my caseworkers at the Commission, though.

"I went back over your file," she said, "and your income is just over the limit at which we are allowed to help you out on this stuff."

"Okay."

"So you should probably just go up to the Lighthouse and pick up a CCTV system for yourself."

"Right."

No wonder the Commission was at war with the Lighthouse, which was at war with the American Foundation for the Blind, which was at war with the Associated Blind, which was at war with the Commission.

"How are you dealing with the glare?" she asked.

"It's noticeably worse." Even with the brim of my hat pulled low, it was now almost as hard to go out in the bright sun as it was to go out at night. "It's getting pretty bad."

"Maybe we should arrange for some sunglasses for you."

"Why don't I just take care of that myself?" I didn't want to imagine the brouhaha if I let these groups try to arrange for some shades. "The doctor right around the corner from me is a low-vision specialist. I've been seeing her for six years. She'll set me up just fine."

There was a pause, and a riffling of papers. "We've already determined that she is not on our list."

"I thought we determined that she was."

"Her office in Queens is, but not her Brooklyn office. No, I'd want you to go back to our doctor on Forty-third Street, that way we'd cover it for you."

"I'll just go buy myself a pair of sunglasses and be done with it."

"But proper sunglasses can run you a couple hundred dollars."

"Not if I get them at Coney Island. I can get a nice pair down there for five bucks, easy."

She told me she'd make an appointment with the doctor on Forty-third Street and get back to me with the details. I was lost in all this, a bottle bobbing free in the middle of Lake Geneva, buffeted by forces I could neither see nor control.

Later that week Marcy phoned to let me know that since the Commission wouldn't cover the cost of the closed-circuit TV, I should come and buy one for myself, simple as that. Simple as that. The truth is, I didn't even want the damn thing. My desk was small, and already cluttered with phones and a computer. I hardly had room to bang my head when I needed to. I sure as hell didn't need some box that would take up what little space was left.

"That's super," I told her. "Why don't I pop up there right now and get one? Cash on the barrelhead."

I knew she was only trying to help. Helping blind folks out was her job. That was fine, but this bureaucratic foolishness was all so aggravating I couldn't help being short with her.

Two weeks later, the Commission lady called to let me know that someone had turned in a used CCTV. I was free to have it on long-term loan. "You'll have to come here, and we'll have someone show you how to install it and use it," she told me. "Then you can take it away."

"I can't do that. I cannot leave work to do that."

"Well, figure something out." She hung up.

I sat at my desk and stewed. It wasn't worth it. None of this. It wasn't worth getting so wracked up by this CCTV thing. Marcy was trying to help, I knew. But she and the others didn't listen. They couldn't take a hint. I wanted to be left alone. I had finished my training, knew how to tap my cane properly, knew how to bake myself a nice casserole. What more did I need? What more did they want from me?

After all the time it took me to ask for their help in the first place—beginning years earlier, with my humiliation at the hands of the social worker who was obsessed with my drinking—and after the speed with which these people had pushed me through the system, finding me my Cane Lady and my Home Survival genie in a matter of weeks, instead of the months it might have taken, you would think I would be grateful, and I was. This on-going benevolence, though, was only frustrating.

I refused to think of myself as a cripple, except if I was looking for some cheap sympathy. My battered pride was holding together, but I wasn't a noble type, and never would be; I would never carry my head high in the face of adversity. I was only trying to deal with this in the best way I knew how. Even though I was no saint, I wasn't all that bad. Losing my sight hadn't changed me all that much.

Dammit.

Suddenly, I didn't want their help anymore. I didn't want much of anyone's help anymore. I would do okay in this world all by my lonesome. As the lights faded faster and faster, I wanted to get on my tricycle again, gather momentum, and ride it headlong into a brick wall, then pick myself up, get back on, and do it again.

getting hip to
the lights-out way

DESPITE THE TRAINING, and the past injuries and humiliations, I found it difficult to get into the habit of pulling my cane out when I needed it. *I can handle this,* I would think when confronted with a darkened street. I continued thinking that way until I got into trouble again.

I was stumbling home late one night, my vision even blurrier than normal. I was proud of myself after slowing down enough to maneuver without incident around a bunch of voices blocking the sidewalk. I was proud of myself for maintaining my balance after hooking my leg on a gate someone had left open. Pride was what kept me from pulling the cane out. I could handle things just fine without any props to declare my cripplehood to the world. Then I stepped on something.

The dog—it sounded like a big dog, too—let out a yelp and jerked its leg from beneath my shoe.

"Christ, didn't you see it?" an old man, the dog's owner, shouted at me.

I stopped, thought about my situation, then turned in the direction of the voice.

"Jeez, I'm very sorry . . . fact is, I *didn't* see it."

"It's a big damn dog!"

"I'm sure it is. I'm sorry. Y'see, this is my fault, see, I have"—I flipped my bag open and reached inside—"I have this red-and-white cane here that I really should be using." I took the cane out and held it for the man to see. "I'm blind, sir. I didn't see the dog, and it was my fault."

"Oh my God. I'm sorry." The anger was gone from his voice, and he touched my arm lightly. "I . . . I didn't know."

"It's okay. There's no way you could've known. If I'd been using the cane the way I was supposed to, you would have, and this wouldn't have happened."

"I'm so sorry." He started to cry, quietly. I felt like a shit.

I squeezed his hand, apologized again, repeated that it was all right, then slid the cane into my bag and shuffled down the last block home, where my cats would know well enough to get the hell out of my way.

A few weeks later, I was in a similar incident. I was supposed to meet some people at a bar after work. They were coming from various parts of the city, and I decided to grab a table early and wait for them. I'd never met some of them before, and I was nervous. It was a reasonably well lit bar when the sun was out, which is why I chose it. That and the fact that the bartenders knew me.

When I walk in from the street, no matter how well lit a place is, my eyes take a few minutes to adjust. And despite the windows, there was a spot of perpetual darkness in the middle of this bar that always gave me trouble. Upon entering, I put my head down and started shoving my way to the back. It seemed pretty empty. Then I stepped on something. Again I heard a yelp. Again I'd stepped on a dog, again a big one.

"Didn't you see him? Open your fucking eyes!" a woman sitting at the bar growled.

Nearly the same exchange followed as with the old man, except that this woman was not at all forgiving. "Watch where you're fucking walking."

"Fine," I muttered as I turned away. I continued muttering

as I stomped to a table in the rear, where I slapped my bag down and yanked out my cane and laid it in front of me. I jammed a smoke in my mouth and sat down to calm myself before going to get a beer.

I was half pissed at her for yelling at me and for letting her dog sprawl across the floor. But I was also half pissed at myself for fucking up again.

As I sat there stewing, the bartender quietly explained the situation to the woman. When I got up and felt my way to the bar, the woman leaned in my direction and apologized.

"It's okay," I told her. "You didn't know."

Then she kept apologizing. When I went to the bar to order a beer. When she passed me on her way to the bathroom. When she passed me on her way back from the bathroom. This went on a long time.

She's been in the bar since then, always with some large beast, and every time I walk past she tugs the creature out of my path.

"See, I pulled him out of your way," she says.

"Thank you, that's very kind. Appreciate it."

When I run into people, or step on their pets, or slam into garbage cans, stoplights, or I-beams on subway platforms, people who see me must assume that I'm intoxicated. Of course they do. Without my cane flopping around, what other explanation could there be?

"Don't laugh at me."

I knew it wasn't coming out loud enough for her to hear me. I didn't care. I stood at the corner, waiting for the light to change, quivering with an old hatred, muttering blood.

"Don't laugh at me."

It was an accident, and a simple one at that. Could happen to anyone; unfortunately, it usually happened to me. I was walking home, it was a reasonably early winter evening, and I bumped into her. Some big woman blocking most of the sidewalk, yapping with some big friend of hers.

I stopped and immediately apologized. It was reflex now. "Excuse me, I'm terribly sorry," I said, trying to look in her general direction, "but I don't see very well."

There was silence, as I shuffled the few yards to the corner. The walk sign was never with me when I needed it. With that sixth sense we blind folk develop, I could feel her tiny eyes on me. I wanted to get away.

The woman started laughing at me. The cruel, subhuman laughter of a junior high schooler. Her friend joined in. They were enjoying my predicament.

I stood on the corner, coward that I was, muttering, "Don't laugh at me," knowing they would never hear over the passing traffic. A few days after the fact, it might be no big deal, but at the time it could only trigger bad memories. I remembered one fall night a few years earlier in particular.

I was in Manhattan, on my way to a club where I was supposed to sing with a band, when a hipster walking a few steps behind me began tossing out insults. I'm not sure why. I tried to ignore him. I had to get to the club, and he wasn't worth it. But it was late and I hadn't taken my anticonvulsive. His comments burrowed into my flesh. I felt tension building in my head, and without any calming intervention, it would probably lead to a seizure.

His insults continued as we reached the middle of the block. I turned on him and threw a roundhouse his way, which caught him on the side of the head but glanced off uselessly. He backed off, stepped around me, and kept walking. I stood in the middle of the cold sidewalk, my rage all but dissipated with that one foul swing.

I could see that he was expecting me at the corner, staring at me as I stood motionless and waited for the fire to go out before I went on to the club. I don't know how long I stood there. Finally the cold started getting to me, and I had to move on. He was still waiting. There was no avoiding it. When I got up to him, I made an even greater mistake.

"Sorry about that," I said. "About punching you in the head."

"Man, I don't get that at all." He chuckled.

He moved on down the street, and I stood there, feeling filthy for having been the coward. First for not doing more damage, and then for apologizing for the damage I had done.

Since then I've had the seizures under control, as long as I remember to gobble my pills. The night those women laughed at me, I almost ran home, away from their mocking laughter, hating them, hating everyone else who had ever laughed at me. I muttered loud enough that folks on the dark sidewalk cleared a path.

Throughout my life, I realize, I've recognized things in myself that were worth mocking. I started mocking them before anybody else had the chance. What's more, my own mockery was much crueler and colder and funnier than anything anyone else would ever dare say.

That made things much easier for everybody.

I never could stand to be laughed at. That's why my encounter with those two women got to me the way it did. They didn't know me, had not read any of my stories, had no clue as to what the score was, or that I would gladly laugh at myself before they had the chance. This was a simple misencounter, the sort of thing that happened to me every day, and I made a kind and quick apology for having failed again. And they laughed at me anyway.

I had had enough.

EVERYBODY I DEALT WITH, myself included, thought it would take a major event to make me use my cane the way I should. Maybe a broken leg or another concussion. Blood would have to be spilled. Instead, all it took was two middle-aged, porcine gargoyles laughing at me on a darkened street corner. The night after that incident, I slipped my cane out of my bag to help me find the way home from the subway, and I've done so since.

I've kicked myself on an almost nightly basis for not having done this before. Using the cane, the very cane I went through six weeks of training to learn how to use, was the best damn idea I'd had in a long time, and for a very simple reason.

By pulling the cane out of the bag and letting it flubbity-flop open, I changed the nature of the game entirely. I inverted the rules. For the past several years, I had been shuffling down the street with all the grace of a crippled lamb, always on the defensive, afraid of what each step would slam me headlong into. I dodged shadows, but plowed straight over garbage cans. I stepped on animals, I stepped on people, and then had to explain why. I was yelled at, I was laughed at. All because my pride kept me from admitting that I needed to use a tool. I was refusing to use a hammer to pound nails, insisting that my forehead did the job just fine, thanks.

But now, ha, now once the cane comes out, I'm the one in control. Tapping home from work just three or four nights after deciding to use the cane, I stumbled hard into three people before I even got to the subway and *they* apologized to *me*.

Suddenly everybody wanted to be nice to me, either by getting out of my way or by offering assistance (which I tend to decline politely).

One day I was crossing a street in the rain and heard two voices nearby. I wasn't sure they were talking to me until they repeated themselves.

"Hold there. Puddle! Big puddle in front of you!"

It was an Australian couple. I hesitated before taking another step.

"Go to your left a bit," they suggested, so I did. "There's still a puddle there, but it's not so big."

I could sense them standing there, cheering me on, afraid to simply reach out and lead me around the damn thing. Maybe they were afraid they might catch whatever I had.

"There you go, straight ahead now. Step up!"

I, of course, dropped my foot into the middle of the smaller puddle, but that was okay. Once on the curb, I started to turn the corner.

"Whoa there, look out! You want to go straight? It's over here."

"No, that's okay." I gestured with the cane. "I'm just going into this bar here. There is a bar here, isn't there?"

I thanked them and waved in what I believed their general direction before going inside.

I HAD BEEN TALKING to friends about this decision of mine, this next step in accepting the present and the inevitable. Discussing matters of pride and self-sufficiency. For a long time, friends had been telling me that it was something I had better start doing. Still, as pigheaded as I am, it was a decision I had to make for myself.

All these months and years, I simply stopped listening to them when the question came up. Once I made the decision to use the cane, however, I could start listening again, happy with myself all the while.

"You talk about pride in making it around without it," one of my friends said, "but there is also a certain pride that must come with using it."

"Everybody parts in front of me like the fucking Red Sea, that's for damn sure."

"Yeah, it's like walking through a crowd with a shotgun."

"Except with a cane, all I can really do is whack 'em around the knees and ankles."

After the *New York Press* offices moved from SoHo to Chelsea, I was forced to walk down Twenty-third Street every morning to get to work. And every morning I would encounter three or four other blind folk. I passed by the Associated Blind building, an apartment complex designed specifically for people who can't see at all. I am told it's a hotbed for carnal rutting-about of every variety. Great orgies of the blind, I hear. And when I see these people tapping down the sidewalk or being led by their guide dogs, I can't help thinking, as I try to envision these orgies, that it's a good thing these people are blind. It's funny how many of them end up looking exactly the same: short, squat, bad bowl haircuts, puffy down jackets, puffier pasty faces. None of them I saw wore shades; I suppose they were content to face the world with their creepy blind stares.

I noted the various cane styles these folks used: they scraped their canes lightly this way and then maybe that, slid along walls, missed beats, simply didn't put their canes to any real, worthwhile use at all. Each person with his own style, but each style too sloppy.

Of course, if they were getting around okay, that was all that mattered, I suppose. Maybe my newfound pride had me working a little arrogant. They should be wielding their canes with determination and cold viciousness, I thought, each tap an announcement that something mean was coming through, so clear a path. Use the thing as if it had a silver wolf's-head handle, and walk tall. These people shuffled down the street the way I used to without a cane, afraid of what every step might bring.

I still feel uncomfortable around the blind. Not horribly uncomfortable, but vaguely so. Not nearly as uncomfortable as I felt around the deaf or the retarded, though. They have always made me nervous. I should know better. But it seems a normal, visceral human reaction to cripples, regardless of the fact that I was one of them.

One night as I was leaving work, I stopped, as I usually did, outside the doors of the office building to light a smoke. I heard a voice next to me.

"You wanna give me a little room, or what?" It was a woman's voice, and it startled me.

"I'm sorry, ma'am." I reached into my bag and grabbed my cane, then let it flop open. "But I didn't see you there."

"Goodness sakes, look at you. You carry yourself just like a sighted person. I think that's great."

"Thank you, ma'am," I said, before heading off down the sidewalk. I took it as a tremendous compliment. Perhaps I shouldn't have. I spent most of my life sighted, or reasonably so, and never had anything but trouble.

"VEER TO YOUR RIGHT A LITTLE."

I recognized the voice by now. This was the third night in a row that I'd heard it. Each time I was tapping my way to the subway after work, and each time it offered some helpful information. Whoever was speaking—it was a man, that's all I know—never stopped, never introduced himself, never spoke more than a sentence, always kept walking.

The first night it was, "You're crossing Twenty-fifth Street."

"Thank you," I said, as we went in opposite directions. By now I was used to people offering helpful bits of information to me. But this guy kept popping up.

The next night it was, "Hurry, the light's going to change at any second."

"Thank you," I said again. And again, I thought nothing of it. It wasn't until after the third night, when he said, "Veer to the right a little," that I came to expect him, and started to find it all very funny and peculiar.

I can't get to the train these days without having one person, and usually more, offer assistance in some way. Whether it's the old woman who told me the light had changed, but to watch out for "those goddamn cab drivers," or the Puerto Rican midget who helped me cross for six straight blocks, or the bum who, goodness exploding from his tattered insane heart, grabbed my arm and dragged me across the street after I told him I didn't need any help, me stumbling over my own feet, the cane catching every bump in the road and finishing in a puddle, the bum furious because I wasn't moving fast enough. Well, I wasn't moving fast enough because the wind was howling that night, and along with handling the cane, I was trying to keep my hat from flying away and to balance a smoke with my free hand as he yanked me between the cars.

In the midst of all these other voices, there has been this singularly kind and accurate one. Even if I didn't need it, even if I knew very well that I had to veer to the right a little, I appreciated it.

THE PHONE RANG in the middle of the afternoon one Tuesday in March.

"Jim?"

"Yeah." I recognized the voice; it was my caseworker from the Commission for the Blind.

"I was concerned," she said. "Jack from the Lighthouse said he's been trying to get hold of you, but you weren't returning his calls. And when he called the paper, whoever answered the phone told him you were just a free-lancer."

"That was him? Yeah, that was me who told him that. He never told me who he was, so I never told him who I was."

"He says he has some computer software tips for you."

"Yeah, well, I'll tell you, when he stopped by the office, oh, what? about eight months ago now, he said he'd get back to me the next day. Never heard a peep out of him, till now. I've since taken care of most of that stuff for myself."

"What did you get?"

I ran through the list. Not too much, but more than the Lighthouse had been able to help with.

"And it's working okay?"

"Yeah, fine."

"Good, then. It sounds like things are going pretty well for you. It sounds like you're doing just fine."

"Guess so," I told her.

"Super. In that case, I think I'm going to close your file. I think we've taken care of everything."

"Yeah, great," I said. "Go ahead."

"Great."

Before she hung up, though, before she could slap a sticker across my folder, happy to have foisted another self-sufficient blind man onto the streets of New York City, no burden on anyone anymore, I stopped her.

"Hey, before you go."

"Yes?"

"Thanks for the help."

"No problem." End of conversation, and I went back to work.

IN ONE OF THE NEWSLETTERS I received regularly from the Lighthouse, someone suggested, as a helpful New Year's resolution, "Update your will." I wasn't sure how to take that when I first read it. I thought it was funny, in a sick way. I still do.

Going blind is itself a sick and funny business. Especially going blind slowly, over thirty years. I got used to the notion as the lights dimmed. It may have taken me a long time to learn to do things, learn to use the cane for instance, but I finally did learn. And I finally did use it.

Blindness, without question, changes a lot of things, despite what all the Blind Man Trainers in the world would like to say. Life becomes much more structured, much more organized, much smaller, at least if you live alone. You can't go out and take a long, aimless stroll through the city on a carefree Sunday afternoon. Okay, you could, but probably not without dire consequences. You can't hop a bus and ride to a town you've never visited, simply because you've never visited that town before. Even the notion of moving into a different apartment, for me at least, is ridiculous. Every object around you must remain cemented in place except while in use. Out of necessity, the blind become in a sense not only agoraphobic but obsessive-compulsive as well.

People who are involved in the blind industry, the trainers, the social workers, the self-righteous types, don't care to hear things like this. But I prefer being honest.

Blindness is a big pain in the ass. If I had a choice, of course I wouldn't be blind. It would be stupid to choose blindness. Given that I don't have a choice in the matter, given that I am in it now, and in it for good, I have to decide where to go from here. Suicide no longer interests me. Nor do I have any interest in being one of those overcompensatory types who learns how to ski and sky-dive. Nor am I interested in joining the blind subculture, full of blind people talking about blind things all the time, wasting their days wallowing in memories of sight.

There is another route, somewhere between denying and wallowing. Despite everything, going blind hasn't bothered me so much, except for those times when I fall or unduly burden someone. It's another thing to deal with, like madness or drunkenness or crime or poverty or the realization that I've hurt people around me over the years. All of those things, in one way or another, will be with me forever, near the surface. Going blind, curiously, has been my salvation from many of these things—or my karmic retribution. The blindness will be *on* the surface, of course, affecting everything I do.

It's just one more float in the weirdness parade I have been marching in my whole life. I know there is more weirdness along the way, around the corner in front of me, so I will trudge along as I have all these years. I'm anxious to see what's coming next. And what's coming will be interesting, that's for damn sure, because I'll keep fucking up. I know I will. It's what I do best.

acknowledgments

Each of the following people has been an essential cog in the machinery of this book, and I thank them all most heartily. My apologies to those I've forgotten. I'll feel foolish when I'm reminded who they are. Lord knows they'll let me know about it.

Derek Davis, my dear friend and first editor, published my first story in Philadelphia's *Welcomat*. Then my second, and my third, and so on for six years. He stood up for me against maniacal publishers, accepted me as one of his family, and taught me how to write.

Ken Swezey and Laura Lindgren have been looking out for me since I arrived in New York. I still don't know why. They've pulled me out of hospitals and taken me to some strange places. If not for them, I wouldn't have connected with *New York Press* and wouldn't have written this. Their comments on and criticisms of early drafts of the book were beyond helpful. I owe them very much.

Laura L. Koenig, a wonderful poet and playwright, was with me, much to her chagrin, through many of the adventures here. Though our marriage didn't last, I'm proud to call her my friend. She could have left me to die a dozen times, and may have been tempted to, but she didn't. I wish her only the best.

John Strausbaugh, a good friend as well as my editor at *New York Press,* is a straight dealer who has stood up for me dozens of times. He is a man I listen to and trust.

Russ Smith, editor in chief of the *Press*, took a chance,

perhaps against his better judgment, when he brought me aboard. He's quietly taken similar chances ever since.

I tip a great big whiskey to Sam Sifton, formerly one of my editors at the *Press.*

My fellow Guggenheimers worked diligently to keep one another—and me—sane, both inside that beautiful hell and outside: Linda Hunsaker, John Graz, Sue McGuire, Erik and Phaedra Davidowicz, Jim Wallerstein, and Steve and Simone Duresis.

David E. Williams's morbid, disturbed, and lovely music (as well as his friendship) have changed the way I look at the world.

Ken Siman made a phone call one day that, to our surprise, paid off.

David Groff, my editor at Tarcher/Putnam, is a wonderful and slightly twisted man whose suggestions about this book were invaluable. He put up with a lot of foolishness and busted his ass, all with the patience of a saint.

Anna Jardine, the copy editor, went three steps beyond.

Mary, Bob, McKenzie, and Jordan Adrians keep me humble.

Joe Coleman, a man of frightening talents, has always watched out for me.

Greg Sandow first suggested the possibility of a book years ago.

My illustrators—Russell Christian, Marcellus Hall, Bob Hires, Carol Lay, Tony Millionaire, and Takeshi Tadatsu—and the *New York Press* staff, past and present—including Kevin Baier, Murray Cockerill, Greta Cohen, Michael Gentile, Don Gilbert, Adam Heimlich, Lisa Kearns, Adam Mazmanian, and Al Nesselt—deserve my thanks, as do Jeff Koyen and Amy Nathanson for technical support.

The people at Buffa's helped keep me under control and well fed five days a week.

acknowledgments

And the following have always been kind to this cranky sum'bitch: Jim Caufield, Desire, Homer Flynn, Hardy Fox and others at Cryptic, Genghis, the Hangdogs, Gordon Kato, Don Kennison and Ann Walton, Corrine Kurie, Louise Paluzzi, Adam Parfrey, Clayton Patterson, Frank Petito, M.D., David Read, Jean Rosenthal, M.D., Suzanne and Peter Ross, Celso Vera, Mike Walsh, Gretchen Worden, Andrea Zimmerman, M.D.; the fine folks at the Khyber Pass Pub, Moby Dick's, 288, and Botanica (Jay!); the magazines and whatnot that have published my stories; and the other writers at the *Welcomat* and *New York Press.*

Finally, Morgan Intrieri's loving enthusiasm and endless support have made writing this book much easier. I owe her many beers.

about the author

Jim Knipfel lives in Brooklyn, with beasts.